The *Farscape* Episode Guide for Season One

An Unofficial, Independent Guide with Critiques

by Talis Pelucir

Lightning Rod Publishers
Bremerton ⍾ Port Orchard ⍾ Tahuya ⍾ Seattle

The Farscape Episode Guide for Season One
An Unofficial, Independent Guide with Critiques
copyright 2000 by Talis Pelucir
published by Lightning Rod Publishers

ISBN 1-883573-56-4
First edition March 2000
Second edition March 2001
Third edition December 2002
Fourth edition April 2004
9 8 7 6 5

Cover by Tom Gibson

All rights reserved, including the right to reproduce this book or portions thereof in any form whatsoever, except in the case of short excerpts for use in reviews of the book.

Printed in the United States of America.

For information on reprint and other subsidiary rights, please contact Mari Garcia at mgarcia@windstormcreative.com.

Lightning Rod is the pop culture and Internet division of Windstorm Creative, a multi-imprint, international organization involved in publishing books in all genres including electronic publications, producing games, toys, video and audio cassettes as well as producing theatre, film and visual arts events. The wind with the lightning bolt center was designed by Buster Blue of Blue Artisans Designs and is a trademark of Lightning Rod Publishers.

Lightning Rod Publishers
c/o Windstorm Creative
Post Office Box 28
Port Orchard WA 98366
farscape1@windstormcreative.com
www.windstormcreative.com
360-769-7174 ph.fax

All Farscape properties © 1999 The Jim Henson Company, SciFi Channel, Nine Network Australia and Hallmark.

This book has not been prepared, approved, licensed, endorsed or authorized by The Jim Henson Company, SciFi Channel, Nine Network Australia or Hallmark. It is a scholarly work of criticism, an independent, unofficial publication.

Lighting Rod Publishers is a member of Orchard Creative Group Ltd.

Dedication

To the cast, creative team and crew.
But especially, to Cee.

Acknowledgments

Thanks to everyone at Lightning Rod, especially Jennifer and Cee, and to Tom Gibson for the fantastic cover.

The *Farscape* Episode Guide for Season One

An Unofficial, Independent Guide with Critiques

by Talis Pelucir

Table of Contents

Preface	11
Premiere	13
I, E.T.	21
Exodus from Genesis	24
Back and Back and Back to the Future	29
Throne for a Loss	33
PK Tech Girl	37
Thank God It's Friday... Again	42
That Old Black Magic	47
DNA Mad Scientist	52
They've Got a Secret	56
Till the Blood Runs Clear	59
Rhapsody in Blue	64
The Flax	68
Jeremiah Crichton	72
Durka Returns	76
A Human Reaction	81
Through the Looking Glass	85
A Bug's Life	90
Nerve	95
The Hidden Memory	100
Bone to Be Wild	105
Family Ties	111

Preface

Regarding Critiques
and the Official Episode Guide

As you're reading my critiques, please remember: *I really love this show*. The critiques are my personal opinion based on my background as an author and a teacher of literature and drama. So my "take" on the episodes is going to come from a storyteller's perspective, a literary perspective.

As a published writer, one of the first aspects of a TV show I look at is the plot. Have I read or seen this before? Where? If so, why have the writers chosen to use the same basic storyline here? What does it reveal about the characters? Where does it work? Where doesn't it?

Because I've read so much science fiction, fantasy and world mythology, I sometimes become impatient when writers on any particular show don't stretch their creative muscles enough to present us with something new. But I also understand that what they write as well as what is presented is governed not just by their own inspiration and understanding of the characters and show's premise, but also by viewer feedback via various media (including BBoards), advertising dollars, the producer's vision, the director's vision and more. The actors, like the writers, often don't have much control — if any — over what happens to the characters. Ratings are big business and big money and if a show wants to stay on the air, everyone involved will try to hit the largest demographic in order to keep it going.

This sometimes means that the premise of a

particular episode, or in some cases a whole series, will be based on a formula of what has worked before. And that's okay. I understand how the industry works and luckily, *Farscape* doesn't often fall into these traps.

Lastly, let me say again that these critiques are only my opinions. You will certainly have your own. Sometimes you will agree with me and other times you won't. And that's exactly as it should be. This is one of the main reasons Lightning Rod Limited publishes unofficial critique guides — because they are full of honest opinions not influenced by the numerous pressures I mentioned earlier.

However, I do encourage all readers to purchase the Official *Farscape* Episode Guides because they will most likely offer behind-the-scenes or "insider" information that an unofficial guide cannot. Additionally, you can check out *Farscape! The Best Websites and Factoids* which will lead you to the most unique *Farscape* websites on the Internet as well as provide you with loads of trivia about the show. You'll find a lot of different opinions of the episodes on the web as well as places you can share your own thoughts about the show.

Episode 10101: Premiere
Location: Uncharted Commerce Planet
Cast:
Ben Browder as John Crichton
Claudia Black as Officer Aeryn Sun
Anthony Simcoe as Ka D'Argo
Virginia Hey as Pa'u Zotoh Zhaan
Jonathan Hardy as voice of Dominar Rygel XVI
Lani John Tupu as voice of Pilot
John Eccleston, Dave Collins, Sean Masterson, Graeme Haddon and Tim Mieville
as movement for Rygel & Pilot
Guest Cast:
Kent McCord as Jack Crichton
Murray Bartlett as DK
Lani John Tupu as Bialar Crais
Christine Stephen-Daly as Lt. Teeg
Damen Stephenson as Bio Isolation Man #1
Colin Borgonon as PK Weapons Officer
Writer: Rockne S. O'Bannon
Director: Andrew Prowse.

SYNOPSIS:

While human astronaut John Crichton prepares to test his theory of using the Earth's gravity to propel him into faster-than-light travel, in the proverbial galaxy far far away three prisoners break out of their cells and release Moya, a living ship, and her symbiotic Pilot. As they struggle to remove Moya's Control Collar, their Peacekeeper captors send out Prowlers to recapture them.

In the midst of the ensuing battle, John Crichton emerges through a wormhole he unwittingly created during his experiment. Colliding with an attacking Peacekeeper Prowler, his ship spins momentarily out of control. Soon thereafter, he's pulled into Moya's cargo bay. Disembarking, Crichton makes his way to command. There, he sees his first two real aliens: Ka D'Argo and Zhaan. D'Argo, menacing and enraged, is shouting in a language he can't understand and Zhaan is . . . well, blue. While trying to communicate with them, he's injected with translator microbes by a bug-like robot that scoots along the floor.

Peacekeeper Officer Aeryn Sun's Prowler has also been pulled aboard Moya. Crichton finds himself in a holding cell with Officer Sun. She mistakes him for a fellow soldier; he assumes she's Human.

Shortly thereafter, Officer Sun is exiled from the only life she's known among the Peacekeepers when her commanding officer, who also happens to be Bialar Crais, declares her contaminated due to her prolonged contact with the aliens aboard Moya. Additionally, Crais calls Crichton his blood enemy since Crais believes Crichton is responsible for the death of his brother, Tauvo, when *Farscape 1* collided with Tauvo's ship. Eventually, they elude the Peacekeepers and return to Moya and flee, but now all are on the Peacekeeper Most Wanted List. These unlikely traveling companions must form an uneasy alliance. Their very survival depends upon it.

CRITIQUE:

Pilot episodes are always difficult — not just to write, but to produce and critique as well. The writers have to establish their characters, their setting and the basic conflicts, all in the space of about forty-six minutes. The viewers must immediately identify with the "human factor," and main character, John Crichton. His relationship with his best male friend as well as his father, his lack of a love interest, his well-honed physique balanced against a sharp intelligence, his willingness to take personal and professional risks — all these factors create a likeable if sometimes arrogant human male who personifies a certain archetype in science fiction. He's the young, good-looking pilot, the hotshot with a vulnerable side who's going to have to think on his feet in this new world.

Pitted against him are an array of recognizable, yet familiar characters — archetypes all — who will form his new "family." The attraction between Crichton and Peacekeeper Aeryn Sun, established in the premiere, will provide the show's underlying sexual tension which the writers will both develop and let simmer. This familiar formula (think Mulder & Scully) will generate enormous fan attention and fan fiction (for those who want all the ellipses of this relationship filled in.) Although Aeryn is Sebacean, there is enough physical similarity between the two races to make her attractive to Crichton, and therefore, by extension, to the audience. She's an intriguing mix of tough warrior (she's hardly ever seen without a pulse rifle) and woman (long, dark hair which is often left loose). The so-called "golden audience," which is primarily men between 18 and 35 years of age will identify with John and desire Aeryn and this is an important marketing tool which will help ensure the health of the show.

Like John, Aeryn suddenly finds herself on the outside of her culture — an unwitting exile from everything she's ever known and all of her expectations of what she thought her life would be. Unlike the three prisoners, Pilot, Moya, and even Crichton to a certain extent, who all knew the events of this day would change them, Aeryn's day started like any other. She certainly didn't expect, at its close, to find herself cut off from her Peacekeeper family. If she even knew how much the other races hated the Peacekeepers, she'd probably never experienced that hatred in such a personal way before. Captured, imprisoned on the other side of the bars, she's immediately suspicious, aggressive and looking for someone to blame. Crichton, the unwitting cause of her predicament, is the perfect target. This initial chemistry — the image of Aeryn sitting on Crichton's chest and beating the heck out of him is forever burned onto our retinas — is a great way to setup the uneasy love/hate relationship that will follow.

The other characters are equally as interesting and engaging. Dominar Rygel XVI is a cantankerous, self-important, arrogant, pain-in-the-behind whose desire to put himself first will give us lots of character conflict and also comic relief. Created by Brian Henson, voiced by Jonathan Hardy and operated by John Eccleston, Dave Collins, Sean Masterson, Graeme Haddon and Tim Mieville, he's fantastically realistic. Throughout the series, it's actually hard to remember that he's not "real," so phenomenal are his facial expressions and movements.

In this same vein, Pilot, who is operated by John Eccleston, Dave Collins, Sean Masterson, Graeme Haddon and Tim Mieville, and voiced by Lani Tupu is also a fantastic creation. The symbiotic relationship he shares with Moya is fascinating and we're immediately curious about where he came from and how he came to be joined with Moya. And although we won't see how large he actually is until later in the first season, we do become aware of his multiple "arms" and his bug-like shell and "hat." What helps us to identify with him immediately (especially in the face of films like *Starship Troopers*) are his very recognizable facial expressions and sensibilities.

Pa'u Zotoh Zhaan is an interesting choice in terms of the group's makeup. Once a warrior, now a priestess, Zhaan is a complex mix of calm spirituality, sensible reactions and female sensuality. In many ways, she's Aeryn's opposite — she exudes a definite femininity, despite her willingness to be aggressive in a pinch. She's assertive where Aeryn is aggressive which provides a female/male polarity between the two female characters, and she is be more the peacemaker, the go-between and mediator of the group's conflicts. She also is set up initially to function as the group's moral compass. We identify with her because her ethical code is recognizable to John and therefore to the audience.

Ka D'Argo may or may not be Crichton's ally. He's the only other humanoid male, but he's also got a chip on his shoulder the size of a house. Distrusting, aggressive, he seems destined to kill either Crichton or Aeryn. Casting Anthony Simcoe, who is noticeably taller than any of the other actors, was a great choice here. Simcoe's imposing physicality heightens his character's aggressive nature and he does a beautiful job of infusing D'Argo with classic warrior qualities: Unwavering courage in dangerous situations, an incredibly high tolerance for pain (the metal rings imbedded in his torso were put there by the Peacekeepers sans anesthetic because handcuffs and a collar were not enough to restrain him), the willingness to take risks which may be physically dangerous, the kill-first-ask-questions-later mentality, and a deep hatred for Peacekeepers which fuels his anger and informs his decisions. Although he seems almost stereotypical, there is more to him than first meets the eye. As with Aeryn and Zhaan, he is in opposition to Crichton. Where Crichton is more likely to stop, think and analyze, D'Argo is more likely to act.

Taken as a whole company, we find each of these characters an outsider in her or his own way. All are far from their homelands, friends and family. The setup, which echoes the familiar story of a hero trying to find her or his way home, is easily recognizable.

The show also offers some familiar motifs in terms of science and general archetypes. In terms of the science, creating a bio-mechinoid — a living ship, as Moya is called — is a choice that will provide lots of opportunities for conflict and plot development. Unlike a mechanical, soul-less starship (like Aeryn's Prowler or Crichton's *Farscape 1*), Moya has a will of her own, as well as desires, fears and other emotional responses to the situations the crew find themselves in. Her pregnancy and the birth of the offspring, Talyn, at the end of Season One, will inform the crew's decisions throughout the first season as they are sometimes forced to choose between the offspring's safety and their own desires.

The translator microbes are also a neat way to deal with the language barriers bound to exist between cultures and races. Although we are treated to the sound of D'Argo and Zhaan's "true" voices for a brief moment in the pilot episode, it isn't until "A Human Reaction" that we really get to hear what the characters sound like sans translator microbes. And unlike the translation program that fueled the *Star Trek* universe, which was a good idea, but was unrealistic in some situations, the injection at birth scenario raises some interesting questions about how the races in this universe are bound together — who came up with the microbes? How are they distributed? Manufactured? Controlled?

The archetypal setup of renegade band of fugitives running from large corporate-type evil pursuer is pretty standard fare, not just in science fiction. The question of whether or not this will work as the premise will play itself out over the course of the series, but as a framework, it's definitely tried and true. Crais and the Peacekeepers, and later Scorpius, give something for the crew to metaphorically push against, providing conflict and fueling the storyline.

And, as we shall see by the end of Season One, it's hard sometimes to tell who your friends are and who are your enemies. The creative team doesn't opt for any easy outs here and the shifting alliances within the crew throughout the first season will prove quite interesting.

ONE TIER BELOW:

- The ring Jack Crichton gives his son, John, will appear again in this season's final episode, "Family Ties."
- Peacekeeper culture is extremely strict about contact with other species. The "irreversible contamination" which condemns Aeryn to exile is one of the ways the Peacekeepers keep their ranks pure.
- The rings embedded in D'Argo's collar bones are not part of his warrior markings, but were put there

by his Peacekeeper captors in order to chain him to the wall.
- The tattoos on D'Argo's chin are the marks of the general he once impersonated.
- Rygel would be considered a political prisoner as he has been imprisoned because his cousin seized the throne and deposed Rygel. Both D'Argo and Zhaan seem to have committed crimes, though we don't know what they are yet.
- The fact that Sebaceans and Humans appear very similar raises one of the series' basic questions: What is the connection between these two universes?
- When the animatronic Pilot was completed and the puppeteers climbed inside for the first time, Pilot fell face first onto the floor and had to be repaired before shooting could continue.
- Rygel is manipulated both by puppeteers in physical contact as well as by remote control.
- All of Rygel's dialogue is added later.
- Aeryn Sun is the name of a computer company in Australia.

Grade: A

Episode 10102: I, E.T.
Location: Uncharted Planet Dena
Guest Cast:
Mary Mara as Lyneea
Cayde Tasker as Fostro
Boris Brkic as Ryymax
Mark Shaw as Alien Soldier #1
Dominic Bianco as Alien Hunter #1
Heath Wilder as Alien Hunter #2
Writer: Sally Lapiduss
Director: Pino Amenta

SYNOPSIS:

The newly escaped prisoners soon realize that Moya is transmitting a homing signal which will bring the Peacekeepers down upon them if they can't disable it. The attempt to remove the device, called a Paddac Beacon, not only causes Moya great pain but also is unsuccessful. The crew decide to take refuge on a nearby planet where Moya can partially immerse herself in swampland to dampen the signal.. The choice of an Earth-like planet seems a good one until Crichton is separated from the others and encounters a well-meaning scientist who's been listening and watching the skies for contact from "aliens" her whole life.

While he attempts to win her trust and find the chemical compound called Clorium which acts as a numbing agent and will relieve Moya's intense pain, Aeryn and D'Argo are literally treed by a bunch of "rednecks" searching for the aliens they're sure have landed. Meanwhile, back on the ship, Zhaan, Pilot and Rygel attempt to calm Moya. This is the first of many episodes where Rygel, because of his small stature, is forced into Moya's inner reaches (this time it's her neural nexus) to remedy the problem. His inept attempts to remove the beacon provide both the comic relief and the escalating conflict.

Crichton is eventually successful, returning with the Clorium. The surgery is completed and Moya lifts herself from the swampland moments before her own bulk would have crushed her in the planet's gravity.

CRITIQUE:

This episode, unfortunately, draws too heavily on some of the old familiar motifs in science fiction and fantasy, most of which have already been fully explored. The connections here between works like Steven Spielberg's *E.T.* are unfortunately obvious. Crichton bonds with the single mom who believes in UFOs and whose work is monitored, and therefore controlled, by the government. In order to escape, he has to get her to trust him — and win her son's trust as well. Additionally, Crichton's temporary position as positive male role model bonding with the fatherless boy covers no new ground. The farewell scene and the episode's final tag in which the mother and child talk about how this encounter will be the stuff of family legend is overly melodramatic.

Although Moya is in danger, the focus is more on Crichton's predicament and the other characters are overshadowed by what is known as the "A" Story (Crichton as alien). The subplot, or "B" Story (Moya in danger; the others' attempts at gathering materials to help), becomes all but buried.

As the second episode, this was predictable. The writers have to firmly establish Crichton as a fish-out-of-water and show him connecting with other outsiders in an easily identifiable storyline. Because we are trained to root for the Extra-Terrestrial, we root for Crichton, thus establishing our bond with and empathy for the main character.

It does, however, set up a few interesting ideas. First, we've seen Crichton-as-alien in the pilot episode and we identify with him, maybe even asking ourselves how we might react in a similar situation. Second, in this episode, he has to convince Lyneea and Fostro that neither he nor D'Argo, who he barely knows and is as foreign to him as he is to Lyneea and Fostro, that he and D'Argo are, in effect, the same. This allows him to form the beginnings of an alliance with D'Argo as a male friend. Finally, it firmly establishes Moya as a living entity, an essential member of the cast of the show.

ONE TIER BELOW:

- Clorium's anesthetic properties will figure prominently in a multiple-episode story arc in Season Two.
- This is the first of several episodes in Season One in which the discovery of Peacekeeper technology aboard Moya will have an adverse effect on the crew.

Grade: C

Episode 10103: Exodus from Genesis
Location: Uncharted Space Cloud
Guest Cast:
Damian de Montemas as Melkor
Jodie Dry as Kyona
Geoff Barker as PK Commando #3
Chenoeh Miller as PK Commando #4
Tai Scrivener as PK Commando #5
Writer: Ro Hume
Director: Brian Henson

SYNOPSIS:

While hiding out in an asteroid field to evade a Peacekeeper Maurader scout, Moya is invaded by something. That something is raising the ship's internal temperature (like The Borg *in Star Trek: First Contact*) and creating replicants of John, Aeryn, Zhaan and D'Argo. For a while, all the clues we get are images of giant bug-like creatures running through the halls and stealing objects which will provide them with the crew's DNA. But for what purpose? The crew's first inclination is to fight back, but this only results in the temperature rising — an outcome that proves quickly deadly for Aeryn Sun. Sebaceans can't process any external heat which raises the body's core temperature. In other words, they don't sweat like we do (although they do seem to perspire). And they don't pant either. So while Aeryn succumbs to a brain fever which will eventually become the Living Death, the others attempt to find and remove the invaders.

When Zhaan is pierced with a sharp-ended projectile, she gains the ability to communicate with the alien race, the Draks, who reveal that they have come into the ship to breed and require heat to do so. Rygel, who has been sent into the ship's nether reaches again, is eventually embraced as the crew's emissary. All struggle to find a way of preserving both the breeding cycle and Aeryn's life. But in the meantime, they're stranded in space and are boarded by Peacekeeper Commandos from a Marauder scout ship. These newcomers don't know anything about the cease-fire agreement between the passengers and Draks and when the Peacekeepers begin killing the replicants, thinking them the real prisoners, the Draks assume the peace has been broken.

To disable the Peacekeepers, the companions agree to raise the ship's temperature, hoping to induce brain fever in the invading troopers, but risking Aeryn's life in the process. While Aeryn and Zhaan share a shower scene that is probably going to be one of the most downloaded bits from the series, Crichton and D'Argo battle the Peacekeepers and defeat them. Against D'Argo's better judgement, Crichton convinces the others to let the Peacekeepers go. With them he sends a message to Bialar Crais: It was an accident.

CRITIQUE:

This is really the first episode where we see a more standard ensemble approach to storytelling. Here, each character has his or her part to fulfill in the larger story and the screen time is pretty much balanced between them.

For the first time, we see Aeryn move from toughness to vulnerability and there are several poignant scenes where she struggles with her growing inability to function. She loses motor control and then her memory begins to be affected. When she begs Crichton to kill her if she enters the Living Death, we see the possibilities that exist between them.

Aeryn also chooses her outlaw companions over her old life with the Peacekeepers. Knowing the elevated temperature will disable the PK troops, she agrees to raise the heat rather than risk the troops gaining control of the ship.

Several long camera shots of Aeryn, prone and shivering on a bed, begin to create the allure of Aeryn as an object of desire — for both Crichton and the viewers. She's strong, yet vulnerable. She can't do it all herself, as much as she'd like us to think that she can. And Crichton, in agreeing to kill her if necessary, takes the first step toward integrating her into the crew. Even Pilot is frightened and fascinated by her. It's probably Zhaan, however, who takes the greatest personal risk in terms of embracing Aeryn — literally — holding her up in a cold-water shower as Crichton and D'Argo go after the Commandos.

We learn a little more about each of the characters in this episode. For example, when Rygel is hailed as the group's leader by the Drak "mother," it furthers his role as savior-with-a-comic-twist. In D'Argo's case, we see his warrior-sensibility come into play (as well as his dreadful lack of experience) when he suggests everyone cut off the tip of his or her smallest finger to distinguish their true selves from the replicants. Luckily, that's not what they decide to do. Pilot pushes past his fear of the Peacekeepers when he allows Aeryn to be in close proximity — and it's here we get a sense of how large he really is for the first time. For Zhaan, it's the ability to serve as a conduit for another race, an ability often associated with advanced spiritual practices (or back-room psychics — take your pick).

And last but not least, Crichton is set up as the idea man. The average guy who comes up with sensible solutions. Although it's a comic dichotomy to see him get his butt kicked by his own replicant (and hear his self-deprecating remark about his lack of down-and-dirty fighting skills), this only reinforces the female/male polarity that exists between Crichton and D'Argo. And taking this one step further, it sets up the feminine-man/masculine-woman interplay between Crichton and Aeryn.

In a powerful and beautifully shot ending scene, Aeryn and Crichton have their first meaningful, if awkward, conversation. Aeryn teases him and he laughs at himself, endearing him to both us and Aeryn.

In terms of developing the world of the Uncharted Territories, D'Argo introduces Crichton to Dentics, which look like giant raw Black Tiger prawns and are used to clean one's teeth. Pay attention to the way Crichton dresses and grooms, especially throughout the first season. He's unkempt — hair, beard and fingernails in particular — until he gets the hang of living in this new world.

There were a few bumps, though. One could argue that this plot device has been overused — see *Dr. Who: Invasion in Time* for an example of a second threat behind the first one — and that the real threat is never adequately addressed. Why do the Peacekeeper troops collapse so quickly when Aeryn, who's been out of formal PK "training" for a while, manages to survive quite a bit longer? Oh, and one last thought ... does anyone remember the film *Enemy Mine*? Interestingly enough, the lizard-like race in that film was also called

Drak. It makes you wonder sometimes if it's like the street name phenomena — there are only so many names to go around and we just keep reusing them.

ONE TIER BELOW:

- The fact that Sebaceans are heat intolerant will continue to figure prominently in the show, especially for a character we won't meet until the end of Season One.
- Rygel's "small" stature works in his favor here as he's the only one who can fit into the passageways which lead to the chamber the Drak mother has chosen for giving birth.
- Zhaan's ability to tune into other beings and act as a conduit are the result of her priestess training.
- The fact that Crichton convinces the others to let the Maurader troops live sets up the power dynamic between him and the other crew members which will provide some rich character conflicts as the show progresses.

Grade: A-

Episode 10104: Back and Back and Back to the Future

Location: Uncharted Territories: Ilanic Cruiser
Guest Cast:
Lisa Hensley as Matala
John Clayton as Verell
Writer: Babs Greyhosky
Director: Rowan Woods

SYNOPSIS:

Two travelers with a secret are welcomed aboard Moya. D'Argo's obvious attraction to Matala and support of Verell sets him apart from the crew immediately. D'Argo believes they are trustworthy because Ilaics are distant genetic cousins to the Luxan race. Crichton keeps having flashes of the future. At first, they're wholly sexual and he's confused by the fact that Matala seems bent on seducing him. When he tries to talk to D'Argo about it, he's met with animosity and the ugly side of male competitiveness over a desirable female.

Talking with Zhaan, Crichton begins to gain some insight and finds that in order to break the chain of events which seems destined to occur, he must make different choices. He starts by breaking a lovely glass mask in Zhaan's quarters.

In the meantime, Aeryn follows a hunch about Matala and challenges her to a friendly sparring match. When Aeryn's knocked unconscious by what seems like a variation on the Vulcan neck pinch, Aeryn's suspicions that Matala is really a Scorvion who's been surgically altered to look Ilanic are confirmed. Since Scorvions are enemies of both the Ilanic and Luxan races, we wonder what Matala is up to and what Verell's secret project is all about.

The more suspicions are raised, the more aggressive Matala becomes. Crichton's premonitions that their visit will result in tragedy seem unavoidable. Crichton, knowing that he is the only key to changing the outcome, finally succeeds. Verell is killed; Matala escapes in the ship with the secret weapon which turns out to be a "contained" black hole. She is destroyed, ultimately, by the weapon she coveted.

CRITIQUE:

Confusing in parts and obviously sexually charged, this episode relies too heavily on explicit sexual content to boost ratings. I wondered about the appropriateness of some of Crichton's premonitions, especially those that contained the not-so-subtle suggestions of Matala showing Crichton a "good time." My neighbor, who's ten, watches the show and I don't think his father was too thrilled about having to explain what was implied.

Although one could argue that this story is a time-tested formula to attract male viewers, one can also see it as the mark of a lazy writer to fall back on this idea. Additionally, how uninspired to rely on the stereotype of a woman using her sexuality to get what she wants, whether it's D'Argo's cooperation or the weapon for her people. In any case, the episode didn't impress overall. Crichton's role as the one who figures it all out is already a cliche and doesn't do justice to the other characters' intelligence. Granted, he's the one having the premonitions, but writer Babs Greyhosky makes him inarticulate enough, especially with Zhaan, to ensure he's going to have to go it alone for most of the episode.

D'Argo fairs pretty well here in terms of character development. His admission that it's been a very long since he's been intimate with a woman augments his loneliness. Additionally, Aeryn has a terrific fight scene.

Some will argue that the fast pacing of the episode and the constantly shifting futures keeps the viewer glued to the screen until the outcome. But too many questions remain: Does Matala intend to keep Crichton off-balance by sending him sexual images? Why does she only send images to him? Why doesn't she send non-sexual but equally confusing images to Zhaan or Aeryn? If the others have suspicions that she's not what she seems, why does the story focus primarily on Crichton? Does the flash-forward effect just "wear off?"

The answers to some of these questions may lie on the cutting room floor (or in the writer's original script), they're missing from the final cut. Pay attention here, too, to the connections to other scifi: The black hole in the center of the ship in *Event Horizon*, which also had terrible ramifications for the crew or the use of the alternative time-line in "Cause and Effect" (*Star Trek: The Next Generation*) and "Visionary" (*Star Trek: Deep Space Nine*).

ONE TIER BELOW:

- Aeryn is able to discern Matala's true race because of a particular movement she uses when fighting.
- If you look closely and remember the Peacekeeper symbol displayed on the floor of the sparring room, you'll get an early clue to the powers behind the root

harvest in "Thank God it's Friday... Again."
- D'Argo's impulsive nature and lack of life experience, two of his primary character traits, are highlighted in this episode.
- This is Rowan Woods' first outing as a director for this show.

Grade: D

Episode 10105: Throne for a Loss
Location: Uncharted Jungle Planet
Guest Cast:
John Adam as Bekhesh
Jeremiah Tickell as Kyr
Zoe Dimakas as Hontovek
Api Bavadra as Nonk
Writer: Richard Manning
Director: Pino Amenta

SYNOPSIS:

Rygel steals one of Moya's crystalline components in the hopes of establishing a trade agreement with the Tavleks. Unfortunately, the Tavleks make their living raiding and kidnapping. Thinking Rygel might actually be worth something, they kidnap him and hold him for ransom.

Although some of the crew argue for leaving him, the problem is that Moya can't break orbit without the crystal, so rescue is the only option.

In the skirmish to grab Rygel, a young Tavlek soldier is captured by the crew. While Aeryn, D'Argo and Crichton take his armor and Gauntlet to deal with the problem of Rygel's rescue, Zhaan stays aboard to help the soldier deal with the withdrawal he experiences from the sudden loss of the Gauntlet. When worn on the forearm, the Gauntlet punctures the skin and provides a constant supply of a performance-enhancing drug. Even though Zhaan treats him with respect and tries to show him that life always provides choices, he fights her at every step and eventually returns to his people and his addiction.

Planetside, Aeryn, D'Argo and Crichton each

take a turn wearing the Gauntlet, which helps them eventually free Rygel although it exhausts each in turn. Reunited finally on the ship, Aeryn waits impatiently for Rygel to "retrieve" the crystal which he has swallowed and once she has it in hand, he tells her he "thinks" he remembered to wash it.

CRITIQUE:

Generally a well-paced and well-written episode. The three storylines run smoothly in tandem without leaving the viewer feeling confused.

The poignant scenes between Zhaan and the young soldier are very well done. When he mocks her body, she drops her robes for him, leaving him — and many of us — slack-jawed. She also shows her warrior background and her physical strength when he tries unsuccessfully to overpower her. The sense of failure and disappointment she feels when he chooses the drug over his new found self-awareness is heartfelt and well acted.

This storyline had resonances in *Star Trek: Deep Space Nine's* Jem Haddar, a race of warriors bred (like Peacekeepers) to fight, who are also addicted to a drug early in their lives which sustains their aggression and ensures their loyalty.

The story also serves as commentary about the ultimate futility of trying to help someone who isn't ready to change.

Wisely, writer Richard Manning uses the Aeryn/Crichton/D'Argo plot mostly as comic relief. Watching the characters perform in almost superhuman ways and then collapse into immobile puddles is damn funny at times. Certainly the scene between Crichton and the

Tavlak in which Crichton realizes the drug in the Gauntlet is gone is a classic "oh, shit" moment

Although Rygel's imprisonment has its frightening moments, his overblown sense of self-importance has become a permanent character trait — one that both serves him and gets him into a lot of trouble. But probably the funniest scene has to be the one in which he hands Aeryn the crystal and the look of absolute disgust on her face when she realizes that he might not have bothered to wash it after it was expelled from his nether end.

ONE TIER BELOW:

- Zhaan's incredible physical strength is displayed here when she overpowers the Tavlak soldier.
- Zhann's blood is white and she is able to "puncture" herself without sustaining long-term physical damage. For a humanoid such as John or D'Argo to do this would be self-defeating, and yet Zhaan doesn't hesitate. This scene hints at Zhaan's origin and provides one of the many clues dropped about her race in Season One.
- Zhaan's blood has healing properties.
- When Luxans are injured, their blood flows black. In order to be able to heal properly, the Luxan must be pummeled until the blood runs clear. Aeryn's knowledge of Luxan physiology gives us an indication of how far-reaching Peacekeeper culture is even as it startles John to see her pounding on D'Argo's wound instead of binding or applying pressure.
- Rygel's impulses to put his own needs first will continue to be a point of conflict among the crew.

- Bekhesh will make an appearance again in Season Two.

Grade: A

Episode 10106: PK Tech Girl
Location: Destroyed Peacekeeper Carrier, the Zelbinion
Guest Cast:
Alyssa-Jane Cook as PK Technician Gilina
Derek Amer as Teurac
Peter Astridge as Lomus
Peter Knowles as Evran
David Wheeler as Captain Durka
Writer: Nan Hagen
Director: Tony Tilse

SYNOPSIS:

When Moya comes across the devastated remains of the Peacekeeper carrier *Zelbinion*, it means different things to different crew members. For Aeryn, it's a reminder of everything she's lost and she experiences genuine homesickness as she and Crichton board the craft. For Rygel, it's a frightening reminder of his early imprisonment and the time spent under the charge of the sadistic Captain Durka. The others see an opportunity to salvage whatever might have been overlooked by those who attacked the *Zelbinion* in the first place, including maps to the Uncharted Territories.

When Crichton and Aeryn board the ship, they find Gilina, a Peacekeeper Technician who's been sent by Bialar Crais on a salvage mission. Attacked by the fire-spitting Sheyangs, who are bent on gutting the *Zelbinion*, Gilina is the only survivor of the PK crew. She informs Aeryn that Aeryn's entire regiment had been demoted after her defection. This doesn't endear her to Aeryn and it's made worse by the obvious and sudden attraction Gilina and Crichton feel for each other.

The Sheyangs return, forcing D'Argo and Zhaan to stall for time or risk being destroyed. Rygel, after a discussion with Zhaan, sets out to find Durka's body in order to confront his memories and unburden himself. Gilina proposes using the *Zelbinion*'s Defense Screen to prevent the Sheyang from gaining access to the ship and protect Moya from attack as well. Just before the Screen becomes active, one of the Sheyang warriors manages to board the *Zelbinion* and Gilina and Crichton are saved at the last possible moment by Aeryn. The Sheyang withdraw. Gilina opts to stay aboard the *Zelbinion* to await the Peacekeepers' return.

CRITIQUE:

Although this episode heightens the sexual tension between Aeryn and John, the piece isn't particularly interesting in terms of the timeline of the show or in exploring new avenues of the *Farscape* universe. The "time-out" for love in the face of possible annihilation is silly and some of us may share Aeryn's obvious annoyance at Gilina and Crichton's adolescent antics, especially when she comes upon them kissing while she's busy hauling equipment from one part of the ship to another.

While American viewers might marvel for a moment at the fact that Sebeceans kiss the eyebrows first instead of the lips (common practice between lovers in Australia), most of us will just groan at this attempt at exotic foreplay. If the intent was to remind us that Humans and Sebaceans are similar, we get it already. Although it's important to keep Crichton and

Aeryn's attraction for each other alive in viewer's minds, showing attraction through jealousy isn't particularly interesting.

D'Argo is really the only character who gets a chance to stretch here as he uses his physical presence and bravado to buy time. While Zhaan's ability to think on her feet adds a nice dimension to the development of her character, the tension between them is not sustained throughout. D'Argo ends up sounding whiny while Zhaan comes off as controlling and pushy.

Personally, while the idea of being able to spit fire was a cool trait, I found the Sheyang's infighting tedious and predictable. These characters had the potential to be truly frightening as the mere thought of being turned into a crispy critter is pretty scary for most of us. But since we know the heroes will survive, there's no real threat inherent in the plot. It would have been a more complex choice for Gilina to hold the panels instead of Crichton; then Aeryn's arrival at the last moment would have had different implications. To have her save Gilina would have been a far more interesting choice.

It was also unrealistic for Crichton to physically hold the panels apart, given the much-discussed attraction they'd have for each other. But since the writing in this episode wasn't subtle, it didn't surprise me that this metaphor wasn't either. Given the powerful connection between Gilina and Crichton, it's obvious we'll see her again, especially since she's already in the Uncharted Territories.

Lest one think I hated this episode, let me say that's not completely true. I loved seeing Aeryn as strong, capable and willing to kick butt. Watching her drop into the melee in the last scene was wonderful. (Anyone catch the line transported from the original *Star Wars* film?)

I also liked the way in which Zhaan used D'Argo's anger to their advantage. Both of these choices were great.

And finally, I was awed by the destruction of the *Zelbinion* given its mythic stature in the Uncharted Territories. Setting up the knowledge of a race more powerful, more destructive and more determined than the Peacekeepers lets us know that this is a dangerous place and the characters would be wise to keep that in mind as they continue their journey.

ONE TIER BELOW:

- Gilina's revelation that Aeyn's entire regiment was demoted after her "contamination" and disappearance is the first news she's had of her former companions.
- The inherent class differences between soldiers and techs is apparent in the hostility between Gilina and Aeryn.
- Gilina will reappear at the end of Season One.
- Crichton is given the opportunity to be the science guy in his interactions with Gilina. His science background hasn't come into play since the first episode when he computed how to bounce Moya off the atmosphere to elude the PK troops.
- Why don't the translator microbes work when D'Argo is initially cursing at the Sheyang?
- Teurac will reappear in Season Two.

- Both Aeryn and Rygel are familiar with Durka. For Rygel, he evokes terror. What he represents to Aeryn will be detailed in the upcoming episode "Durka Returns."

Grade: C

Episode 10107: Thank God It's Friday... Again
Location: Planet Skykar
Guest Cast:
Angie Millikenn as Volme
Ken Blackburn as Hybin
Tina Thomson as Tanga
Selina Muller as D'Argo's Girlfriend
Mark Slocum as Skykaran Male #1
Peter Baroch as Skykaran Male #2
Writer: David Wilks
Director: Rowan Woods

SYNOPSIS:

D'Argo, in a fit of Luxan alpha-male posturing called hyper-rage, flees Moya after threatening Crichton's life. The crew takes the transport pod planet-side to try and find him only to discover that he's found his Eden and intends to stay.

Dominar Rygel thinks someone is trying to assassinate him, but it's really his bodily excretions which have become deadly (as if they weren't bad enough before!). Everything, including his sweat, is suddenly explosive and it's up to Aeryn, with Pilot's help, to find a cure.

While Zhaan and Crichton stay planet-side to try and get D'Argo to change his mind, Aeryn and Pilot quick-freeze Rygel. Aeryn, whose always preferred a pulse rifle to a pencil, must overcome her own self-doubts to save Rygel.

Down on the planet, Zhaan joins D'Argo in the fields harvesting roots for export. Crichton is ambushed by a family who are immune to the root's endorphin-enhancing effects. They draw him into their plot to overthrow the current leadership and break the yoke of slavery these people don't even know they're under.

Aeryn, proud and successful after "curing" Rygel, joins Crichton and together they expose the truth — the Tannot roots being harvested are used by the Peacekeepers to make pulse rifle fuel. This truth does indeed set them free — and D'Argo, Zhaan and the others are reunited on Moya.

CRITIQUE:

A nicely balanced show with both the A (D'Argo, Zhaan and Crichton) and B Stories (Aeryn, Rygel and Pilot) balancing each other. The seed of a potential relationship between D'Argo and Zhaan is presented. Zhaan and Crichton are also "paired" and Aeryn's character is expanded from "chick with gun" to include the intellect many of us were sure she possessed (as a genetically-engineered species, she would have been "bred" for problem-solving on some level) and one of the variations on the classic time-loop scifi plot is explored in a new way.

The acting here is very strong, as is the writing, except for a few minor missteps. More on those in a minute. What works in the story is the understanding that D'Argo's happiness is a false one. Although he's presented as a fierce and angry warrior, we must also remember that he's young by his race's standards. There is a part of him that wants nothing more than to settle down and leave his violent and conflict-heavy past behind.

When Zhaan is also sucked into the illusion, it's not as powerful because D'Argo is so much angrier and dissatisfied in general. This is the first chance we have to see D'Argo as something other than an angry warrior — just as it's our first chance to see Aeryn as an intellectual — and it's really a nice way to continue to develop the characters.

As for Zhaan, this is one of the places where you can see the creative team experimenting with the chemistry among the actors. It's no secret that one possible romantic pairing was between John and Zhaan. One of the episode's great moments is definitely the expression on John's face when he wakes up to find Zhaan's hand resting comfortably on his crotch.

Additionally, the final scene in which Zhaan and D'Argo are sharing an intimate conversation can also be read as a way for the creative team to test audience reaction to various couplings. Although the emotional relationship between D'Argo and Zhaan is given some screen time, the two won't click as a couple and it's pretty obvious that what's sparking is the relationship between John and Aeryn.

There's also a great sense of humor in this episode: Rygel's combustible secretions, Aeryn accidentally breaking off one of Rygel's whiskers and Pilot's recommendation that she be careful of his other appendages are the most noteworthy.

Additionally, the makeup and costume design in this episode are extraordinary. Notice in particular the final scene between Zhaan and D'Argo. Changing D'Argo's color pallet from red to black is a fitting tribute to his state of mind, but it also lends a different feel to the "colors" and overall design of that scene. The reddish skin of the planet-side race with their red costumes against the blue sky and green of the fields contrasted elegantly with their leader's white costume and skin tone and her very strange and spooky eyes. Note, too, the use of red light on this particular character and the way that augments the overall feel of the bar where the nightly celebrations take place.

In terms of red herrings, they're few but important.

First, why did D'Argo fly into a Luxan hyper-rage? Was it just used as a convenient way to get the plot going or is something else happening beneath the surface? This is never adequately addressed because by the time they find D'Argo, he's already under the influence of the root. Second, how does Rygel manage to survive the fact that his excretions are now explosive? How does he sweat and not blow himself up, not to mention relieve his bladder. And finally, the scene between Crichton and Aeryn in which he implores her to "just trust" him when she asks for an explanation of what's going on is the mark of sloppy writing and editing. In the time it takes them to argue, he could have sketched out the basic conflict. There were better uses for the time this scene occupied. The writer dropped the ball here since the silly bickering jerks us out of an otherwise smooth narrative.

ONE TIER BELOW:

- The fact that Luxans can go into hyper-rage gives us some insight into D'Argo's race. The ancient Celts were also famed for their battle rages which, in the case of the Picts, were so fierce that enemies sometimes fled the battlefield rather than engage the seemingly crazed warriors.
- D'Argo's desire to settle down and raise crops will emerge again in Seasons Two and Three.

- John's role as the character who straddles both storylines and has the most information will be often used by the writers as the series progresses.
- The first clue we get about the root's potential uses comes from the fact that Rygel's digestive processes create an explosive substance.
- The insignia located inside the storage facility is the same one on the floor of the sparring room aboard Moya which we saw in "Back and Back and Back to the Future."

Grade: A

Episode 101018: That Old Black Magic
Location: Unknown Commerce Planet
Guest Cast:
Lani Tupu as Bialar Crais
Chris Haywood as Maldis/Igg/Haloth
Grant Bowler as Liko
Christine Stephen-Daly as Lt. Teeg
Jake Blundell as Lt. Om
Wadih Dona as Tauvo Crais
Vic Rooney as Admiral Josbek
Writer: Richard Manning
Director: Brendan Maher

SYNOPSIS:

When Rygel comes down with Klendian flu, Moya and her crew detour to a commerce planet in search of a remedy. In the marketplace, Crichton encounters a motley fool who seems to know everything about him. He lures Crichton into a walled enclosure. There Crichton's taken prisoner by the sorcerer Maldis and set into battle against his fiercest enemy, Bialar Crais. Crais, when he was "taken" by Maldis to fight Crichton, was embroiled in a row with Peacekeeper Central. They want him to abandon the search for Moya — and therefore, also, Crichton. Crais wants to continue.

Zhaan, meanwhile, has encountered spice merchant and once-warrior Liko, with whom she shares an immediate attraction, as well as a love of fine perfumes. When they realize Crichton has become Maldis' prisoner, Liko explains that Maldis is a sorcerer who has gained control of their world. Now he's looking for a ship to take him off-planet so he can expand his powers and continue his conquests.

Crichton's physical body is taken back to Moya. His psychic projection, however, which has taken physical form, continues to battle Crais. Crichton weakens almost to the point of death. Maldis, meanwhile, grows stronger by feeding off the negative energy Crais' hatred creates. Aeryn and D'Argo search for a way into the fortress while Liko persuades Zhaan to embrace her dark side and join with him to defeat the sorcerer.

Eventually, Zhaan and Liko are able to break through Maldis' psychic blockade and make him "real" enough for Crichton to defeat him, although it costs Liko his life. Aeryn and D'Argo gain access to the fortress and in the end, everyone is restored to their bodies and Maldis' essence is scattered in a million particles that will — hopefully — never be able to reassemble.

CRITIQUE:

Like "PK Tech Girl," this is not one of the series' strongest episodes, but it does lay the groundwork for events which will occur later. What's most important here is the insight we get into Zhaan's abilities — and into her past. Although she's said she was once a warrior and she has gained many abilities and insights on her spiritual path, much of who she is and where she's been are unknown to us. The revelation of her psychic abilities, which are substantial, is very interesting and this episode reawakens the darkness inside her which she has worked for years to control.

What doesn't work in her scenes with Liko is his tutoring. Asking her to inflict pain on an innocent creature (forget for a moment that the dual-headed bird is in the marketplace as a culinary delicacy) when their real task is to defeat a morally corrupt sorcerer is a non-sequitur. There is no reason to kill the bird other than to show that Zhaan has a conscience, which has been established previously. Given her experience and training, I was surprised she didn't reject his suggestion as illogical and push him to give her a more appropriate assignment. Using one's fierce, and even animalistic, instincts to help and protect one's friends does not necessarily require a dark night of the soul experience and this aspect of the storyline didn't ring true.

Additionally, Aeryn and D'Argo are completely wasted in this episode. They look like brainless warriors hurling themselves against the unscalable walls of Maldis' fortress. Rygel's Hynerian death-ritual when he's convinced Crichton has died is probably the episode's best scene — although watching Crichton grab (practically by the eyeball no less) and kiss Rygel when Crichton realizes he's alive is a close second.

And as for Crichton, watching him stumble around trying to convince Crais that he's sorry gets old after the first five minutes. Crichton is a smart guy — why he doesn't understand that Crais is not going to be satisfied until he has avenged his brother's death with Crichton's blood? As with "Exodus from Genesis," seeing Crichton as a buff wuss just doesn't work. And portraying him as the sensitive male human in a brave new world only goes so far. He's too easy going when someone is physically attacking him and too prickly when his culture comes into conflict with others'. Although reversing this might be seen as too easy a solution, finding a more comfortable balance would be a nice change.

While Crichton does get Crais to admit that

Farscape 1 was no match for Tauvo's PK Prowler, we're still left with the question of why Crais didn't rewind the "tape" of the collision of the two ships to see it for what it was. We have to wonder what else the creative team is setting us. The character who probably fares best here, aside from Zhaan, is Crais. He emerges as more than a two-dimensional bad guy — a good sign.

ONE TIER BELOW:

- Crais' conflict with PK Central Command is just beginning and will figure prominently beginning with the final episodes of Season One.
- Crais' desire to continue to search for Crichton seems to be based purely on the fact that Crichton is responsible for Tauvo Crais' death. However, there is another possibility which, though not made explicit, exists. Crais saw Crichton come through the wormhole. He may be interested in pursuing Crichton to gain access to the technology he assumes Crichton has and uses his brother's death as a convenient cover story. Additionally, it's possible that Crais is obsessed with or believes he's in love with Aeryn Sun and intends to pursue her.
- Zhaan's training as a Pa'u are explored a bit further here and we learn that she has well-developed psychic abilities. She also struggles with the darker impulses such as the desire to inflict harm, which she clearly does not want to actively embrace or bring to the surface of her consciousness.
- The Hynerian death ritual, with its inventory of goods, is reminiscent of the Ferengi custom of mixing commerce with death. In the Ferengi's case,

desiccated bits of the deceased are sold to the highest bidder and it's considered an honor to own a piece of a well-respected and successful businessman after his death.
- Aside from the other bad guys, we now know that there are also sorcerers in the Uncharted Territories.

Grade: B-

Episode 10109: DNA Mad Scientist
Location: Isolated Inhabited Asteroid
Guest Cast:
Adrian Getley as Nam Tar (movement)
Julian Garner as Nam Tar (voice)
Sarah Burns as Kornata
Writer: Tom Blomquist
Director: Andrew Prowse

SYNOPSIS:

What would you do to get home? That's the basic question that fuels this episode. When Moya's crew hears of Nam Tar, an individual who's willing to trade a map crystal of the "uncharted" territories for a little of their DNA, they agree to meet with him.

At first, it seems like a simple exchange — but the stakes keep getting higher. First Nam Tar only wants a DNA sample, but then he asks for one of Pilot's arms! When Zhaan and D'Argo ambush Pilot and cut off one of his limbs, Crichton is outraged. Pilot, however, is nonplused. He explains how his species has developed a symbiotic relationship with Moya's species in order to explore the universe and also tells Crichton that they are dedicated to service. Pilot holds no malice toward either D'Argo or Zhaan. But Crichton isn't as forgiving.

In the meantime, Aeryn decides to donate a sample of her DNA in the hopes of finding a Sebacean-populated world, but instead of taking a sample, Nam Tar splices some of Pilot's DNA into her genes and she begins to metamorphose.

Nam Tar, we come to see, was once an lab animal whose genetically-enhanced intelligence has outpaced that of his "creator," Kornata. Crichton, once he realizes this, convinces Kornata to help him and eventually thwarts Nam Tar's plans to graft Pilot's multitasking abilities onto his own form, returning him to his original lab rat status. They also find a way to reverse the DNA graft experiment Nam Tar had begun on Aeryn Sun.

CRITIQUE:

This is an amazing episode for a number of reasons. First and foremost, it explores the question of how much each person would risk and/or give up to get home. What it reveals may make us uncomfortable. And that's good. We may not like either Zhaan or D'Argo here, but we certainly understand them better. And while we may share Crichton's righteous indignation for their actions against Pilot, we also appreciate Pilot and Moya's symbiotic relationship on a deeper level.

Aeryn Sun's revelation that she can't go home as easily as any of the others is underlined by her initial revulsion and dismissal of the DNA donation process. She can't return to the Peacekeepers and isn't sure she wants to be part of a civilian Sebacean colony. When she begins to rethink her decision, she doesn't want her vulnerability and loneliness to become public knowledge, so she returns to Nam Tar's lab alone. By that time, Nam Tar has procured one of Pilot's arms. To Nam Tar, Aeryn represents possible freedom — with the help of Pilot's DNA. To the others, Nam Tar embodies Dorothy's Ruby Slippers — he's their ticket home.

When Aeryn begins to change, it's horrifying.

The scene she and Crichton share in Pilot's command center, when she shows him how her body is reshaping itself, is wonderfully realized.

The second reason the episode is truly outstanding is the makeup. Aeryn's transformation is so realistic, so frightening and made all the more real since we know Nam Tar can — and will — imprison anyone by offering whatever s/he most desires. Guest actor Adrian Getley does a fantastic job embodying Nam Tar. The fact that Nam Tar's so physically huge is an incredible plot device. Additionally, Kornata's deformities, especially her huge hands, are the work of gifted artists. But watching Aeryn transform from familiar Peacekeeper to something that's part-Sebacean/part-Pilot is amazing.

This episode has all the ingredients of good science fiction — a believable, realistically motivated plot with logical outcomes and resolutions that's based on scientific fact extrapolated out to the "what if" stage. It also includes a setting familiar enough to grasp but different enough to be unique, and incredible visual effects — this time in the form of makeup and CGI. Of all the episodes we've seen so far, this one focuses on Season One's premise: Travelers trying to find their way home. It also provides insight into the guarded yet budding friendships, shifting loyalties and the willingness to be unrepentant in one's selfishness. The final scene in which D'Argo offers Pilot the only apology he knows how is poignant without being melodramatic — and that's what makes this episode outstanding.

ONE TIER BELOW:

- Nam Tar spelled backward is Rat Man.
- The fact that Aeryn now has some of Pilot's DNA will be further developed as the series progresses.
- This is the first time that civilian Sebacean colonies are mentioned.
- The fact that Aeryn trusts John enough to show him what is happening to her illustrates that she is coming to trust him.
- In Mary Shelly's classic horror novel *Frankenstein*, Dr. Frankenstein's Monster overpowers his creator and escapes to cause quite a bit of harm and chaos before he is recaptured.

Grade: A

Episode 10110: They've Got a Secret
Location: Uncharted Space
Guest Cast:
Alison Fox as Lo'Laan
Grant Magee as Jothee
Writer: Sally Lapidus
Director: Ian Watson

SYNOPSIS:

Complaining that doing a security sweep for leftover Peacekeeper devices is not a warrior's task, D'Argo kicks loose a hidden Peacekeeper conception shield in a fit of Luxan impatience. Not only is he sucked into the vacuum of space, but his perception of reality is also altered once he's revived. He's convinced Zhaan is Lo'Laan, his now-dead wife; Crichton takes on the role of Macton, Lo'Laan's brother, and Rygel becomes Jothee, D'Argo's beloved son.

Unraveling the mystery of D'Argo's past is entwined with the necessity of finding and turning off the Peacekeeper device. Exacerbating this problem is Pilot's sudden and inexplicable illness and the abrupt diversion of Moya's resources to some unknown receptor.

Eventually, D'Argo's wits begin to return. He reveals that not only was his wife Sebacean, but she was also murdered by her brother in an effort to separate the lovers. D'Argo, framed for the murder by Macton, has been imprisoned for a crime he did not commit. Crichton, searching for answers to Moya's inexplicable behavior, discovers she's pregnant.

CRITIQUE:

The pregnancy throws a new ingredient, and an intriguing one, into the mix. This episode also fills us in on the reason behind D'Argo's imprisonment. Although Aeryn's role in this episode is clearly as one of the supporting players, she does provide comic relief by playing the Sebacean form of Twister on the floor when first her foot and then her hand are glued down by some overzealously protective DRDs.

What has been badly handled in other episodes is well done here — the focus is clearly on D'Argo, but all of the other players are utilized equally in their supporting roles. Additionally, what we learn about D'Argo really adds depth to his character and helps us understand his hatred for the Peacekeepers. Macton, his wife's brother, was a Peacekeeper. Macton arranged for D'Argo to be arrested and imprisoned, though certainly the death of his wife was punishment enough for what the Peacekeepers regarded as a fouling of the genetic purity of their race.

The fact that D'Argo is a passionate individual was never in question, but the depth of his passion is neatly revealed when we learn that he gave up his culture and later his freedom to be with a woman he loved. He and Aeryn forge a fragile trust. D'Argo reveals to her that Jothee is still alive. She agrees to keep his secret, despite the Peacekeeper conditioning which values racial purity.

In addition to D'Argo's backstory, this episode is an important stepping stone in the story arc which will occupy the rest of Season One — Moya's pregnancy and the birth of her offspring.

ONE TIER BELOW:

- Luxans can survive for a short period of time in the vacuum of space without having to wear an EVA suit.
- D'Argo was imprisoned for a murder he did not commit.
- D'Argo has a small holograph of his wife and son that he keeps in a secret "compartment" in his chest.
- The story behind the conception shield that D'Argo kicks loose will be told in Season Two's "The Way We Weren't."
- The Peacekeeper's commitment to genetic purity will be an issue that is revisited in several later episodes.

Grade: A

Episode 10111: Till The Blood Runs Clear
Location: Inhabited Dam-Ba-Da Planet
Guest Cast:
Magda Szubanski as Furlow
Jeremy Sims as Rorf
Jo Kerrigan as Rorg
Writer: Doug Heyes, Jr.
Director: Tony Tilse

SYNOPSIS:

Inside *Farscape 1* with Aeryn, Crichton tests out the new enhancements on his flyer. As he harnesses the gravitation forces produced by solar flares and replicates the conditions which created the wormhole that brought him into this universe, he's delighted with the results. A wormhole appears. Unfortunately, it's unstable and as *Farscape 1* catches the edge of it, the ship is damaged by a plasma leak.

Pilot recommends they abandon the flyer, but Crichton refuses. He decides to land on a nearby planet, hoping to find a repair facility. Unfortunately, he asks Aeryn about the decision after he's made it. Her acerbic response sets up the tension which ripples through the rest of the episode.

D'Argo, impatient to put more distance between them and Peacekeeper patrols, argues for abandoning Aeryn and Crichton, but his words fall on deaf ears. Zhaan is more interested in abandoning her clothes than she is in abandoning Aeryn and Crichton and she secludes herself in order to more fully experience the intense "photogasms" the flares induce.

Down on the planet, Crichton and Aeryn cross paths with two Vorcarion Blood-Trackers who are bent on collecting the reward the Peacekeepers have posted for Rygel, D'Argo and Zhaan. When Aeryn interrupts the transmission of the Peacekeeper Beacon, the Blood-Trackers become aggressive and Crichton's only hope at keeping them safe until *Farscape 1* is repaired is to play a delicate game of who's-the-alpha-male with Rorf. Everything seems to be under control until D'Argo's patience abruptly ends. He comes looking for Aeryn and Crichton and is immediately captured by Rorf and Rorg.

In the meantime, Aeryn has managed to get the Peacekeeper Beacon to accept her personal code. It plays a message from Bialar Crais promising her reinstatement and retirement with pension intact if she betrays her companions. Crichton assumes she'll be loyal to them, but she is noncommittal. We're reminded of Gilina's comment (in "PK Tech Girl"): The only way Aeryn's regiment will be reinstated with honor is if she's captured and killed. This raises the question of whether or not Crais' offer is legitimate.

Soon after, while checking on the repairs, Aeryn is attacked by another bounty hunter. Exposed to the solar flares sans goggles, she's blinded during the scuffle. Furlow, the owner of the "garage" where *Farscape 1* is being repaired, kills the bounty hunter and she and Aeryn strike a deal. Furlow manipulates the data inside the Beacon so that it appears the hunt for the three prisoners has been called off. In exchange, she gets the flight data recorder from *Farscape 1*. When Rorf and Rorg realize their prisoner is no longer worth keeping, they abandon D'Argo to Crichton. Aeryn's sight returns and the repairs are completed. They return to the ship.

CRITIQUE:

There are some real pros and cons to this episode. On the plus side, there is some nice development in Aeryn's character. We're not sure at first whether or not she'll accept Crais' offer. When she reveals it's only a deadly promise, we understand she can't return to the Peacekeepers now, even if she wanted to. The guarded look on her face when she receives the message coupled with her absolute helplessness when blinded during the attack by the bounty hunter serve as a nice counterpoint to the way she's generally presented and allow us to see a more vulnerable side to her character.

Crichton's desire to protect his companions and his willingness to induce great pain in D'Argo in order to save him are admirable. We're reassured that he's a "good guy" at heart. But he has his own epiphany when he realizes that he and D'Argo are never going to be friends in the way that Crichton understands male friendship.

Zhaan's photogasms allow us to see her as a sexually mature, sexually aware, desirable female — always a good choice. And the scene in which she pretends to still be naked, much to Rygel's dismay, is a comic highpoint.

Furlow, too, is a great character and Magda Szubanski does a wonderful job with her. She's smart, sarcastic and a fierce negotiator. There are a couple of problems with her, though. The first is that one piece of footage is used twice, making her sound silly and repetitive. Second, her references to twentieth-century Earth culture that seem particularly out-of-context. Finally, Crichton offering Furlow food cubes as payment is offensive. Luckily, her expression is worth a thousand words.

Creative team members have hinted that there is some connection between Sebaceans and Humans, so perhaps Furlow's knowledge of Earth culture is a deliberate teaser. And certainly her knowledge of wormholes and desire for additional technical information raises a few eyebrows.

Additionally, the lighting of the scenes inside the Blood-Trackers' "lair" is dramatic and memorable. The Blood-Trackers' makeup is also fantastic and their throaty, growl-like speech patterns are a good choice for this species. I wondered, however, at the wisdom of making their costumes look so much like traditional Native American garb. Perhaps I'm being too sensitive to political correctness here, but I bristled at the implied connection between the Blood-Trackers' lack of ethics and the American historical portrayal of Native Americans as animalistic savages.

Although not one of the best episodes, "Till the Blood Runs Clear" manages to provide both dramatic tension and character development, not to mention the planet had an outdoor espresso bar, though why anyone would want to drink a mugful of something hot on a desert world is a mystery we will probably never solve.

ONE TIER BELOW:

- This is the first time that another character openly admits to wanting data regarding wormholes.
- Crichton knows that he must ensure that D'Argo's blood runs clear in order for the Luxan to survive. He learned this bit about Luxan physiology in

"Throne for a Loss."
- The fact that Zhaan has such an intense response to solar flares will be more fully explained in "Bone to Be Wild," which airs near the end of Season One.
- This is the first time Crichton has to choose between helping his crewmates and obtaining (or in this case, keeping) information on wormholes. It is a conflict his character will have to confront multiple times.
- Like the Tavkek Bekhesh and the Sheyang Teurac, Rorf and Rorg will reappear in Season Two.

Grade: B+

Episode 10112: Rhapsody in Blue
Location: New Moon of Delvia
Guest Cast:
Darlene Vogel as Alexandra/Lorana
Kate Raison as Tahleen
Max Phipps as Tuzak
Michael Beckley as Hasko
Aaron Cash as Pa'u Bitaal
Grant Magee as Jothee
Robert Supple as Young Crichton
Writer: David Kemper
Director: Andrew Prowse

SYNOPSIS:

When everyone except Aeryn wakes from dreams of past loves, the crew realizes that Moya has gone into starburst to aid another pregnant leviathan. But it's all an illusion, an illusion to lure Zhaan to the New Moon of Delvia.

Once there, we realize that a rebel sect from Delvia has settled on this planet. Zhaan agrees to help their leader, Tahleen, move past her anger at the destruction the Peacekeepers wrecked on Delvia and attain a higher level of spiritual enlightenment. Unfortunately, Tahleen's motives are not pure and during the mental bonding called Unity (think Vulcan mind meld but with cooler graphics) she rips away Zhaan's ability to cope with her darker impulses and takes this skill for herself. This leaves Zhaan struggling with aspects of her own psyche she had finally come to peace with after years of meditation and study.

The secondary story in the episode concerns how several of Tahleen's followers keep Aeryn, D'Argo,

Rygel and Crichton distracted so they won't interfere with Tahleen's plans. For Aeryn, this involves tapping into the self-doubts she harbors about her intellect; D'Argo experiences visions of his son; Rygel finds himself suddenly small and vulnerable and Crichton's memories are altered. Instead of parting ways with his fiancée over a disagreement about whose career was more important, Crichton's new memories find Alexandra at his side. Ultimately, though, Tahleen's followers come to distrust Tahleen's motives and reveal themselves and the deception to Crichton. He destroys an object of power, embodied in an ancient tree, which enables him to aid Zhaan and empower Tahleen's followers to set their small society to right.

In the end, Zhaan, devastated by the loss of the inner peace it had taken seventeen cycles to achieve, abandons not only her priestess' garb, but also her title. Crichton is genuinely distressed by Zhaan's choice and he offers a compromise. They share Unity and Zhaan is able to regain some of her inner peace by seeing herself through his eyes.

CRITIQUE:

Aeryn, Rygel and D'Argo are terribly underused in this episode. While it's interesting to learn what Aeryn and Rygel hold as inner secret fears, the plot device of a power-mad leader using her followers to keep these three occupied while our focus is on Zhaan and Crichton is really not very interesting.

Since the episode focuses on Zhaan and Crichton, it's obvious the creative team is exploring the chemistry between Zhaan and Crichton and how it rates with the viewers. While this story does take their friendship to another level and offers some fascinating insight into Delvian culture, it cheats the ensemble nature of the show.

Aside from the much discussed question about whether Aeryn is wearing Crichton's boxers, she Aeryn doesn't have much to do in this episode except look dumbfounded. The fact that Aeryn is the only one who arrives in command in her underwear even though everyone was roused from sleep is an obvious ratings ploy as were the sexually explicit scenes between Crichton and Alexandra/Lorana.

The use of the device where two people experience the same reality completely differently was also done in the pilot episode of *Star Trek: Deep Space Nine* ("The Emissary") when Sisko sees a devastated planet and Dax a paradise. In both cases, it's a manipulation of the senses and the mind by those with talents beyond what Humans (or Sebaceans or Luxans or Trills) possess or have access to.

Tahleen's command to her underlings to "distract" the seemingly simple-minded came off as the easiest way to push everyone Aeryn, D'Argo and Rygel to the edges of the viewer's focus. In other words, David Kemper couldn't figure out what to do with them. Ultimately, however, he ended up making Rygel, Aeryn and D'Argo look idiotic. An obvious alternative would have been to explore their darker impulses since that is what Tahleen was trying to control in herself. That way, the secondary story would resonate with the primary story and add depth to the episode as a whole.

ONE TIER BELOW:

- In an online interview, Claudia Black responded to the question regarding whether or not those were Crichton's boxers with two words: Commerce Planet. I didn't know Calvin Klein had distribution in the Uncharted Territories!
- Zhaan's crime was the murder of her lover, Pa'u Bitaal.
- Zhaan is a tenth level Pa'u. She began her studies in earnest once she became a prisoner.
- The tree Crichton destroys represents Delvian power. Remember this during "Bone to Be Wild."
- For Delvians, Unity is the most intimate act two people can share. While Crichton understands it to be similar to sex, he cannot truly experience its transcendent nature. During Unity, Delvians are susceptible to psychic rape (as with Tahleen) as well as death (as with Pa'u Bitaal).

Grade: C

Episode 10113: The Flax
Location: Uncharted Territories
Guest Cast:
Rhys Muldoon as Staanz
John Batchelor as Kcrackic
David Bowler as Goon
Writer: Justin Monjo
Director: Peter Andrikidis

SYNOPSIS:

Sometimes, even the seemingly empty void of space is not empty at all. That's what Moya and the travelers discover when both the ship and the Transport Pod that Aeryn and Crichton had been using for a little flying lesson get trapped by a giant mesh grid known as the Flax.

Used by Zenetan space pirates as a way to trap and loot vessels, the Flax seems inescapable, until ex-Zenetan pirate Staanz, a self-styled garbologist arrives.

Aeryn and Crichton are unable to establish communication with Moya. The atmosphere in the Transport Pod, which has become almost pure oxygen, needs venting. John knows how to do it, but his space suit helmet was damaged and is now unusable. Aeryn has a way to temporarily "kill" Crichton and then revive him, but isn't completely sure she can manage the technical repairs. Crichton, convinced she can, agrees to let her inject him with the lethal fluid. She runs out of time before she's able to finish the repairs, but manages to revive Crichton. They have about thirty minutes of breathable atmosphere left with no help in sight.

D'Argo and Staanz, using coordinates Aeryn

sent to them via an emergency beacon, set out to rescue them in Staanz's ship. But when Staanz reveals that he was on his way to loot a Luxan Assault Piercer that was also snared in the Flax, D'Argo tells Staanz to go there first, hoping to find map fibers which might help him get back home. This delay compromises Aeryn and Crichton's chances for survival, but it's a risk D'Argo is willing to take.

Back on Moya, Zhaan and Rygel stall two other Zenetan pirates who have boarded Moya with hopes of capturing the errant Staanz. Rygel, in a moment of brilliance, goads Kcrackic into playing a strategy game with Staanz's whereabouts as the winner's prize.

In the end, Aeryn and Crichton are rescued by D'Argo who finds them in a compromising position; we learn that Staanz is actually the female of his species and interested in sharing more than an adventure with D'Argo; Rygel loses the game, but gives Kcrackic false coordinates and the reunited companions are able to break free of the Flax.

CRITIQUE:

This is one of my favorite episodes. Although Zhaan gets short shrift in terms of screen time, her scenes are memorable. The pacing is excellent, every scene moves the story forward. In the Aeryn/John storyline, their situation becomes bleaker and bleaker, despite their best efforts and our assumption they'll be fine. Aeryn's admission that she revived Crichton because she didn't want to die alone portrays her as vulnerable, but not weak. Thinking they only have a short time to live and so begin throwing off their clothes was a great choice here for a number of reasons.

First, it confirms the attraction between John and Aeryn. At this point, the creative team has made it clear they don't necessarily want to be lovers (look at what the sexual tension between Mulder and Scully did for ratings on *The X-Files*), but they are attracted to each other and finally able to express it. Second, this sequence, which ends with D'Argo practically finding them in *flagrante delicto*, is damn funny.

The D'Argo/Staanz aspect of the plot also has its fair share of comic relief beginning with Staanz dropping his pants to prove his story and ending with the "I'm the female of my species." This twist is probably the most interesting proposition D'Argo's ever had. Thankfully, the writer does not fall into any homophobic pitfalls, but allows D'Argo to be delicate — and dare we say even considerate — in his response. One has to wonder though, why it was necessary to make Staanz female in the first place other than to play the resulting sequence with D'Argo for laughs. Additionally, revisiting the question of how much would one risk to get home serves as a reminder that these characters are all still on their own personal quests, despite the developing friendships.

Rygel's ability to fool Zhaan and some of the viewers as well into thinking he is so easily willing to betray his companions was a great choice here. It initially had us thinking that he is the same old self-serving Rygel, but allows him to have the last laugh — at our assumptions and at the Zenetan's gullibility.

A well-paced balance of drama and comedy, "The Flax" stands out as one of the show's best-written episodes.

ONE TIER BELOW:

- In an *Another Universe* interview, Claudia Black says Aeryn's relationship with Crichton is, at this point, based on adult lust.
- The pirates and the Flax will reappear in Season Two.
- Rygel's fondness for gambling is what sets events in motion in Keith R.A. Candido's *Farscape* novel *House of Cards*. It will also be used as a plot device in an episode in Season Two.
- As with "DNA Mad Scientist," the question about how so many species can live and trade and travel in the Uncharted Territories without maps becomes important . Since the writers are focusing on the crew members' independent quests to return home, the fact that they are unable to procure maps from obvious sources such as Commerce Planets, Staanz's logs, or Furlow who obviously sees a lot of off-planet business is becoming laughable. The reason this region of space is called the Uncharted Territories won't be explained until Season Three, which leaves a lot of time for us to wonder whether our intrepid heroes are a little slow on the uptake.

Grade: A

Episode 10114: Jeremiah Crichton
Location: Uncharted Planet Acquara
Guest Cast:
Natalie Mendoza as Lishala
Kevin Copeland as Rokon
John O'Brien as Kato-Re
Deni Gordon as Neera
Tania Mustapic as Maid
Writer: Doug Heyes, Jr.
Director: Ian Watson

SYNOPSIS:

John Crichton probably never regretted the impulse that took him out for a little joy ride in space more than when he realized that Moya was no longer anywhere to be found. Assuming he's been abandoned, he settles on a hospitable planet, grows a beard and is befriended by the local population including one beautiful local in particular named Lishala.

What Crichton doesn't know, however, is that Moya's starburst was an accident, an unpredictable result of her pregnancy and the crew immediately begins to backtrack in an effort to find him. A quarter of a cycle (about three months) later, they locate Crichton. Rygel and D'Argo shuttle to the planet's surface in order to bring him home. Once there they realize there's some kind of dampening field in place and none but the simplest hand-made tools will function.

Aeryn and Zhaan eventually figure this out as well and puzzle out a way to contact D'Argo, Crichton and Rygel using a beacon. In the meantime, Lishala's growing affection for Crichton has not gone unnoticed by either her would-be suitor, Rokon, or his scheming and manipulative mother, Neera. Goaded into confronting Crichton, Rokon sets a series of events in motion which result in the discovery of D'Argo and Rygel.

For a bit, it seems as though everything will fall apart, but suddenly Rygel is being worshipped like a god and we come to learn that the Acquarians were once Hynerian subjects and have awaited the return of their ruler for time out of memory. Rygel relishes his new-found despotism, but when it comes time for him to perform the ancient sacred ritual, he is completely at a loss. Angered, the locals are about to make Rygel the main course in the next Acquarian meal until he unwittingly triggers the device which brings down the dampening field and saves the day.

Crichton manages to convince Rokon that he is not a rival, but a friend; Neera is discredited and the tribe embarks on a new journey, perhaps even into the stars.

CRITIQUE:

Before I critique this episode, let me say I understand that tried-and-true plots are often the staple of series television, whatever the genre. There are production teams whose sole mission is to make sure the show succeeds — which is what we all want, ultimately. And there are viewers who find the familiar story, no matter how clichéd, fun and memorable; I, however, am not one of them.

This episode was, to me, so offensive that the only reason I didn't turn it off was because I knew I had to critique it. It was reminiscent of one of the worst classic *Star Trek* episodes called "The Paradise

Syndrome" in which Captain Kirk loses his memory on an idyllic Native American-styled world, defeats a rival suitor to win the hand of a beautiful woman, fathers a child and watches his wife be stoned to death because he can't remember the incantation to open the temple door and complete the expected ritual. This plot is as old as storytelling and includes some of the most racist stereotypes on our planet.

As with "The Paradise Syndrome," the native inhabitants of Acquara are people of color who wear brightly-colored clothing, have spiritual practices with obscure origins that seem strange yet quaint to the outside observer, lack even the most basic technology, but nevertheless seem "happy." I found myself cringing when they fall down to worship Rygel. Why? Simple: It's racist.

I suppose I could live with the tired, constantly resurrected plot of handsome outsider wins hand of local beauty (usually tribal leader's daughter), angers handsome warrior male who has been promised local beauty's hand in marriage since they were both children playing in naked innocence, fights for his honor (and hers) and either wins the girl or loses her to her original suitor in a gesture rivaling that of any Round Table Knight. But I can't overlook the "happy darky" motif because it reinforces cultural stereotypes that are inappropriate. Writers should question the way they interpret and use these stories. There's nothing wrong with using a familiar plot to win or keep high ratings. There's nothing wrong with retelling old stories in new ways — we do it all the time. There's nothing wrong with wanting the show to be successful and long-lived, but there is something terribly wrong with portraying people of color as idiots who are willing to follow a false-prophet into oblivion.

In addition to the racist stereotypes, there's quite a bit of misogyny going on here as well. Crichton refers to Aeryn and Zhaan as "the girls," though clearly neither of them are and the writer separates the female and male characters, leaving "the girls" to look worried aboard Moya while the men have adventures and save the world, a tactic reminiscent of the worst of science fiction writing and storytelling in general.

ONE TIER BELOW:

- A microt is roughly equivalent to a minute, an arn to an hour and a cycle to a year.
- The Hynerian empire is so far flung that the rulers, it seems, have forgotten how many worlds they have come to dominate.
- Another *Star Trek* episode that's borrowed from heavily is *Deep Space Nine*'s "Paradise." In that story, a misguided leader creates a dampening field to ensure that the people she's "accidentally" stranded on a primitive world won't be able to leave or develop any form of technology. In this way, she is able to dominate and control them. Similarly, the Hynerians created a dampening field on this world so that the inhabitants wouldn't be able to advance past a certain point until the Hynerians were ready for them to do so.

Grade: F

Episode 10115: Durka Returns
Location: Uncharted Territories
Guest Cast:
Gigi Edgley as Chiana
David Wheeler as Durka
Tiriel Mora as Salis
Writer: Grant McAloon
Director: Tony Tilse

SYNOPSIS:

When Moya unexpectedly starbursts (again), she collides with and damages a Nebari transport. Salis, a Nebari official, appeals to Moya and her crew for help. They oblige, only to learn that one of the passengers is the legendary Peacekeeper Durka, who was Rygel's torturer aboard the *Zelbinion*. Thought dead by his people, the legendary warlord has been "cured" of his violent tendencies by the Nebari and now, at least on the surface, he seems the poster child for the rehabilitated man.

The other member of the crew is Salis' prisoner, Chiana, whose only crime seems to be independent thinking. Her plight catches Crichton's attention and she, in turn, attempts to seduce him in an effort to win him over. When that doesn't work, she escapes her handcuffs and torture collar and makes for the hanger deck to procure a vehicle.

Rygel tries to kill Durka with a homemade bomb. Luckily for Crichton, who happened to be in close proximity, the bomb was too poorly constructed to kill. Unfortunately, it destroys the Nebari reconditioning and Durka's sadistic side re-emerges.

Salis turns up dead. Whether by Durka's hand or

Chiana's, it's not clear. But what does become clear is that Durka is by no means rehabilitated. He reveals that he faked his own death and now intends to finish what he started with Rygel. After that, he plans to starburst, putting as much distance between himself and the Nebari as possible. Aeryn, too, becomes his prisoner and for a time, it is unclear whether or not he will kill them. In an uncharacteristic show of magnanimous behavior, Rygel shifts Durka's focus from Aeryn to himself. Finally able to say everything he's wanted to for countless cycles, Rygel calls Durka's bluff. Then he plays his trump card by revealing that Moya's can't starburst and won't be able to anytime soon as her resources are all going to her unborn child.

Durka, fearing recapture, sets out to destroy Moya's offspring. In the end, he's outwitted by Crichton who almost ends up sacrificing himself to save the others. Chiana, who's been injured in the scuffle, is tended by Zhaan who calls her a "brat." Crichton reads Chiana the riot act and everyone is left wondering whether or not Moya will gain another crew member.

CRITIQUE:

This episode picks up some of the loose strands from "PK Tech Girl," revealing the identity of the race behind the *Zelbinion*'s destruction and bringing the legendary Durka back into the picture. To Aeryn, he's something of a cultural hero and she's initially "star struck" in Durka's presence. In their first scene together, Aeryn gifts us with one of her first real smiles. And although she ends up spending much of the episode on her knees (and not worshiping Durka, either), her loss of respect for Durka is fully realized.

The nuances of facial expression reveal much. While it's clear Aeryn doesn't relish the idea of torture, she won't give him the satisfaction of breaking her.

As in several of the other episodes, some members of the ensemble end up taking a back seat. Neither D'Argo nor Zhaan fare particularly well and Zhaan's catty remark about Chiana being a "brat" doesn't bode well for future interactions. Rygel comes off as a bit more multi-dimensional, though one could read his actions as ultimately self-serving. Crichton, as usual, ends up saving the day, but given the way the plot is set up and resolved, it was a logical choice.

One has to wonder, though, about the hard science behind the final scenes. Was the door between the cargo bay and Moya's main chambers open or closed? If the door was closed, would the loss of atmosphere make it impossible for Crichton to speak? Would he really be able to pull himself back into Moya given such a dramatic and sudden loss of atmosphere? Perhaps the answers to all of these questions is yes, but the point is we shouldn't have to ask. At no point should we be pulled out of the action of the story by distracting questions of whether or not the science behind the scene is solid. Additionally why can Moya detect movement near Crichton when Silas is murdered, but not be able to locate Chiana during the ensuing search?

And there is the question of maps. Why doesn't anyone know where they are when Moya and her crew keep running into people who should have maps. Why doesn't anyone board Silas' ship and take his maps while they're doing repairs? Why doesn't he offer? Why don't they ever take advantage of anyone else's technology to help them at least get oriented in their "uncharted" universe? Obviously, someone must have charted it or there wouldn't be all these people flying around.

Ultimately, the episode is only partially satisfying. Aeryn's scenes stand out as does new character Chiana. Putting someone who shares some of Rygel's sneaky inclinations into the mix makes for interesting possibilities. And the addition of another provocative woman doesn't hurt ratings, either.

ONE TIER BELOW:

- As David Kemper is fond of reminding us, Chiana was supposed to have been killed by the bullet that grazed her in this episode.
- Gigi Edgley and Claudia Black both worked on a series called *Water Rats*, though neither of them guest starred in the same episode.
- The Nebari mind cleansing procedure can apparently be reversed. Although Durka's return to his previous state of mind seems to be the result of Rygel's attempted murder, this is not a believable solution. Additionally, how can a race that can't even keep its most powerful weapon of punishment in service have destroyed a ship such as the *Zelbinion*? Although this is the first time we hear about Nebari mind cleansing, it won't be the last. The next time the issue arises, it will be explained in a completely different way which leaves one to wonder whether the creative team either hasn't decided how to handle this race or is leaving the real explanation for a later date.
- If you look closely, you'll notice that Chiana's makeup is more blue in this episode. She becomes

"greyer" as the series progresses – probably so that the Nebari won't become confused with Delvians.
- Durka escapes, which means he may be seen again.

Grade: C

Episode 10116: A Human Reaction
Location: An Unstable Wormhole

Guest Cast:
Gigi Edgley as Chiana
Kent McCord as Jack Crichton
Phillip Gordon as Wilson
Richard Sydenham as Cobb
Frankie Davidson as Newsstand Guy
Albert Mensah as Dialectic
Andy Cachia as Technician
Selina Muller as Woman on Beach
Writer: Justin Monjo
Director: Rowan Woods

SYNOPSIS:

There's a wormhole. And on the other side of it: Earth. Crichton, believing it's time for him to go home, tries to persuade Aeryn to come with him. She refuses. Reluctantly, he takes *Farscape 1* into the wormhole. After losing contact with Pilot, he shoots through the anomaly and finds himself — home.

But it's not the happy reunion he'd hoped for. Stuck in an isolation tank, Crichton finds old allies have become enemies and the only person he can trust is his father. When Rygel, D'Argo and Aeryn take Moya's Transport Pod to look for Crichton, they're imprisoned and Rygel is "accidentally" killed.

D'Argo swears he'll kill anyone who tries to imprison or move him and Aeryn, both terrified and furious tells Crichton that not even Peacekeepers kill their prisoners just to study them. Crichton is caught between opposing forces — his desire to save his friends and his powerlessness in the face of the Human war machine and Human mistrust. When Aeryn escapes, they flee together.

After a night in a hotel room where Aeryn discovers the joys of beer. She and Crichton are together for the first time. The next morning, Crichton dresses her in arguably the most hideous frock ever made and after a brief goodbye to his father, they begin their lives on the run.

Moments later, Crichton senses that something's wrong. Everyone he sees is familiar to him and he begins to suspect that all it not as it seems. When he breaks through this false reality by doing something he'd never done before (entering the Ladies' loo), he literally opens the door into another realm and the truth is revealed. The begin he thought was his father is actually a member of a race called the Ancients who are looking for a planet on which they can peacefully co-habitate with the natives. Humans, being the unfortunately suspicious creatures we are, don't seem likely candidates. Crichton is returned to Moya with the rest of the crew, who had actually never been harmed.

CRITIQUE:

Overall, a great episode. Although I suspected there was another "truth" behind the façade once Rygel was murdered, I wasn't exactly sure how they were going to resolve the problems until the end.

Although the familiar ground of Humans as intolerant, military-driven, suspicious creatures has been covered before in everything from *E.T.* to *Starship Troopers* to the *Alien* movies, we always hope that things will turn out differently but somehow know they won't. Here, the tried-and-true plotline works because it offers us something in addition to what we already know. In this case, it shows us Crichton's willingness to stand up for what he thinks is right, despite his former loyalties.

It also answers the question about Aeryn and John's attraction. Though as in "The Flax," there was the possibility that the next morning could be the end of their time together.

Scenically, the episode presented a chance to showcase the beautiful Australian locale and the rolling expanse of waves contrasted nicely with the dark, cement-block of the military complex where Crichton and later the others were imprisoned.

Running the "alien" lines backward was great way to illustrate how accustomed John — and the viewer by extension — has become to translator microbes. This choice really worked because it not only allowed us to hear the way everyone sounds without the microbes, but it also allowed the actors to use vocal inflections to convey emotion and meaning in a way that another choice (such as subtitles) would not have. We are reminded this is science fiction and these characters, despite their humanoid appearances, are truly from elsewhere.

This episode is extremely important in terms of what will come after and it not only sets up the four-part season finale, but also the major story arc for subsequent seasons.

ONE TIER BELOW:

- Although it's not at all clear from the broadcast that John and Aeryn sleep together, the screenplay

makes it explicit. The screenplay also includes a morning after scene.
- Aeryn's first experience of rain was not in the original script. However, the day they were scheduled to shoot in Sydney, it was raining so the scene was changed "on the floor" or as they were shooting. Additionally, Aeryn's line about the rain was unscripted, added by Ms. Black during the shoot.
- Some of the outside location shots in this episode were taken around Homebush Bay, close to the converted warehouse where *Farscape*'s studio and offices are located.
- Although the creative team refused to "translate" what Aeryn says to Jack Crichton as they're leaving the hotel room, the script is clear. She thanks him for his help, admitting that John was right when he said Jack could be trusted.

Grade: A

Episode 10117: Through the Looking Glass
Location: Mid-Starburst
Guest Cast:
Gigi Edgley as Chiana
Writer: David Kemper
Director: Ian Watson

SYNOPSIS:

Echoing Pilot's statement in "DNA Mad Scientist" that Moya and Pilot experience a sense of purpose and fulfillment by serving others, Moya becomes upset when several members of the crew talk about departing. Because of her pregnancy, Moya's behavior is sometimes unpredictable and her resources are not as abundant as they had been. Moya tries to prove to her humanoid crew that she is still useful. She attempts to starburst, but runs out of energy in the middle and collides with something unknown.

From one perspective, it seems that D'Argo, Rygel and Aeryn go missing, but we soon see that Moya has been split between four dimensions. The crew members are all trapped in different dimensional rifts. Crichton is the first one to put the pieces of this puzzle together. He finds wormhole-like passages from one part of the schism to the other. Shimmying between these dimensions, he coordinates the efforts of his crewmates in an attempt to pull Moya out of the Dimensional Schism. His efforts are thwarted, however, by an unknown entity which seems to exists in all of the four dimensions.

Although the alien seems initially hostile, eventually, we learn that it is attempting to communicate with Moya and her crew in order to help her re-integrate. Through their combined efforts, Moya is re-integrated in normal space.

CRITIQUE:

There are some real high points to this episode. The story is framed by the group sharing a meal. Crichton's exuberant line about remembering to enjoy all of life's moments sums up his — and our — enthusiasm for the characters and the show. The movement of the camera around the group in the opening sequence is a fantastic setup for the dizziness and disorientation that will soon follow.

The color schemes on each in the four dimensional rifts help keep us oriented and it's interesting and sometimes amusing (as with Crichton's propensity to vomit in D'Argo's general vicinity every time he passes through that dimension) to see how each of the characters reacts to the various dimensions. What causes Crichton extreme disorientation and vomiting doesn't affect Chiana, but the aural discomfort Aeryn and Crichton are able to tolerate is excruciating for Chiana.

Although we know that Moya is a living ship, it's sometimes hard to grasp the idea of an entity that not only exists and thrives in the vacuum of space, but also sustains others lives. The emotions behind Moya's attempt to please her crew is as palpable as is their desire to rescue her. At many turns, the crew has been willing to go without for the sake of Moya's child or make choices which inconvenience or even endanger themselves (as in "Till the Blood Runs Clear") in order to protect the unborn leviathan. This kind of unity underscores the characters' common goal which overrides personal agendas.

Additionally, an episode like this helps integrate Chiana. She's part of the effort here. Whether or not she'll stay a member of the crew is still unclear. On one level, it's simply a matter of viewer feedback — will she reach the demographic she was created for or not? But on another level, her presence will shake things up. Producer David Kemper has commented several times that characters will come into and go out of each other's lives — as in real life. Chiana is the first to arrive and stay for a while, although the precedent for this has already been set with the introduction of Commander Crais and then his subsequent disappearance for much of the rest of the season.

The fact that Chiana is a lot like Rygel will make, as the saying goes, "strange bedfellows." She's going to be able to manipulate objects more easily than he is given her humanoid form, and together they may end up being the "bad boys" of the show. Additionally, the fact that she's played as significantly younger (in terms of maturity level) than any of the other characters may result in her being mentored by any or all of them. Whether she'll bond with Zhaan and Aeryn remains to be seen. It will depend on whether or not the show's creators pit her against Aeryn for Crichton's affections and whether the obviously chilly on-screen relationship with Zhaan thaws.

There are a couple of negative aspects to the episode: Crichton is again set up as the guy-who-figures-it-all-out. While it's understandable that Crichton's role is central — he is the Human, the one the audience members will most easily identify with — it cheats the other characters. It also limits the possibilities of group problem solving an ensemble provides. This leads to the second problem: Character popularity. As we have seen over and over again, especially in the *Star Trek* shows, the more popular characters get more screen time. Notice, for example, how *Voyager*'s Chakotay faded into the background as the show progressed and how Quark, the barkeep on *Deep Space Nine* (originally a minor character) ended up with quite a complicated story arc while many of the other ensemble members were pushed to the side.

Given the attention that the John/Aeryn "romance" is getting from the fans, we have to wonder whether the other characters will experience the same quasi-retirement as their *Star Trek* counterparts. Let's hope not. They're all interesting characters played by talented actors and it would be a shame to waste them.

Finally, the red herring: If each person at the controls was standing in the same place on each of the four Moyas, how did they all end up in different positions when the ship is re-integrated instead of literally part of each other as in *The Philadelphia Experiment* or *The X-Files'* "Dreamland" episodes.

Despite these shortcomings, this is a strong episode and even if we didn't get to taste the blue goo they shared at the day's end, at least we can share in their joy at being alive and together.

ONE TIER BELOW:

- Crichton's need to remember sequences and deliver the information to people in each "version" of Moya is similar to the final *Star Trek: The Next Generation* episode, "All Good Things," where Picard has to do the same thing.
- The opening sequence in which Pilot and Moya are

eavesdropping on the crew's possible plans to depart is reminiscent of the famous pod scene in *2001: A Space Odyssey* where HAL gets a glimpse of what the crew has planned for him.
- Aeryn's ability to ream out the complex set of instructions for reversing Moya's course reminds us that her DNA and Pilot's have been integrated.

Grade: B

Episode 10118: A Bug's Life
Location: Uncharted Space
Twenty Arns from the Peacekeeper Gammak Base
Guest Cast:
Gigi Edgley as Chiana
Paul Leyden as Larraq
Richard White as Thonn
Zoe Coyle as Hassan
Michael Tuahine as Rhed
Story by: Doug Heyes, Jr.
Teleplay by: Steven Rae
Director: Rowan Woods

SYNOPSIS:

Even as far into the Uncharted Territories as Moya has ventured, somehow the Peacekeepers still manage to find them. In this case, they're boarded by a Peacekeeper vessel leaking fuel and a PK crew willing to do whatever is necessary to get their top secret cargo to a hidden Peacekeeper base which — frighteningly enough — is within twenty arns of Moya's current position.

Crichton proposes that he pose as a Peacekeeper Captain with Pilot, Moya, Chiana and Aeryn as his subordinates while D'Argo, Rygel and Zhaan act as prisoners. The ruse works at first. Aeryn befriends the Peacekeeper's leader, Larraq, in an effort to gain more information about the cargo and the base. In the meantime, D'Argo rails against being chained up again — even if it is just for show; Zhaan tries to placate him and keep both him and Rygel from blowing their cover.

Rygel's curiosity about the cargo gets the better

of him and Chiana discovers him trying to break into the sealed container. She proves she's just as crafty as he is when she produces a key she's created. The container doesn't contain the wealth or riches they hoped for. Instead, they release an intelligent virus which quickly jumps from body to body, killing two of the four Peacekeepers within minutes. Virtually undetectable, the virus takes possession of its host and alters the host's behavior within seconds. If unchecked, it can generate millions of spores within an arn.

Several issues quickly crystallize: The Peacekeepers and Moya's "prisoners" must work together to find the virus within its host and stop it; the virus is undetectable until it leaves a host's body and once it leaves a body, the virus won't re-enter the same host. But perhaps most insidious of all is the fact that the Peacekeepers intended to modify the virus and use it as a biological weapon to subjugate large populations quickly and easily.

While Zhaan works to find a vaccine, the two remaining Peacekeepers, D'Argo and Aeryn find themselves in a potentially murderous, guns-drawn face off. No one is willing to be the first to try the vaccine, but not trying it will only get them all killed and release the virus into the Uncharted Territories.

Eventually, the virus finds its way into Larraq and, in an instinctual act of self-preservation, he attempts to flee Moya. In the resulting chase, Larraq stabs Aeryn. While Crichton goes after Larraq, D'Argo tends to Aeryn's wounds.

In the hanger, Chiana manages to jump onto Larraq's back. As he throws her off, she rips his PK identification chip from around his neck. He escapes in the PK craft. It's still leaking fuel so Crichton uses the first stage of Moya's starburst to ignite the fuel and destroy the ship.

Although ultimately victorious, the effect of this episode lingers. The knowledge that a Peacekeeper base lies deep within the Uncharted Territories is frightening, to say the least. In the episode's final scene, Crichton tells Aeryn she was lucky — the stab wound was close to her heart, but didn't pierce it. When Aeryn, who was drawn to Larraq both physically and emotionally, replies, her double entendre shows that the aftershocks of this encounter will be felt for some time.

CRITIQUE:

Another solid episode, overall. The chemistry between Chiana and Rygel works very well in this context. Although Zhaan and D'Argo have smaller roles in the larger ensemble, their input into the whole is necessary and important. Aeryn has an opportunity to pretend — if only for a short time — that she is back in her old life. Larraq is not aware of her expulsion from the Peacekeepers. Crichton's role here as problem-solver is given a new twist when everything falls apart. It's good to see him "fail" on some level and for the others to question the wisdom of following his lead.

Mr. Browder, in an online chat in September 1999 talked about trying to vary the accent he used when Crichton is possessed by the virus, but all in all the use of the accent in the first place wasn't the best choice. Realistically, because the show is shot in Australia, many of the guest actors are going to have accents which reflect either English or Australian backgrounds. Trying to describe some kind of ethnic solidarity here by asking Browder to adopt an accent for his role as a Peacekeeper Captain didn't work. And if one looks back on the various guest actors including the heavily-accented Gilina in "PK Tech Girl" and Staanz in "The Flax," trying to perfect an accent to represent a certain class or race of people simply won't work. The fact that Mr. Browder admits he worked on the accent himself reveals there isn't a language specialist on the set, which would be all but unheard of for a television show. Given this, it's impossible to maintain any kind of continuity, especially when the pool of actors the show will draw on for guest roles will include a variety of accents.

The larger problem, however, has to do with the large number of red herrings in the final cut. Why wasn't he able to contact the Peacekeeper base directly if they only have a fuel leak and not a communication problem? Why didn't Moya's crew take the opportunity to plunder Larraq's ship for maps? Why did Larraq assume that Moya was still in PK control even though her control collar was missing? The fact that these questions are so glaringly obvious is disappointing. Who's responsible for making sure this doesn't happen?

ONE TIER BELOW:

- This chance encounter is as important a piece of the larger story arc as "A Human Reaction." Aeryn's injury at Larraq's hands is the inciting incident for events which will encompass most of Season Two and much of Season Three.
- The identification chip that Chiana rips from Larraq's neck will be very useful in the next episode, "Nerve."
- The fact that Crichton can pass as a Sebacean is important to remember. The fact he isn't Sebacean

is also critical.
- What are the Peacekeepers doing with such a devastating biological weapon? Do they plan to attack another race or species or are they going to offer this "service" to one of their various clients as a way of maintaining order on any given world? Can the virus be altered to target specific species or races? The answers to all of these questions may be revealed as the series progresses.

Grade: B+

Episode 10119: Nerve
Location: Hidden Peacekeeper Gammak Base
Guest Cast:
Gigi Edgley as Chiana
Lani Tupu as Captain Bialar Crais
Alyssa-Jane Cook as Gilina
Kent McCord as Jack Crichton
Wayne Pygram as Scorpius
Paul Goddard as Stark
Imogen Annesley as Niem
Stephen Leeder as Commander Javio
Anthony Kierann as Lieutenant Heskon
Christian Bischoff as Bixx
Pete Walters as Crais' Guard
Writer: Richard Manning
Director: Rowan Woods

SYNOPSIS:

The first of the four-part season finale opens with a terrific boxing sequence featuring Aeryn Sun. So awe-inspired are we by this kick-ass Peacekeeper and her left hook that we're as stunned as Crichton when she vomits blood. Confessing that her paraphoral nerve was severed during Larraq's attack ("A Bug's Life"), she tells Crichton she only has sixty arns to live unless they can get a tissue graft from a genetically compatible donor.

Despite Aeryn's protests, Crichton and the others agree their best bet is to try and find the Peacekeeper base Larraq mentioned. Using Larraq's identification chip, Crichton does his best Peacekeeper imitation and bluffs his way onto the Gammak Base with Chiana as his personal "server" — a.k.a. the sexy distraction.

Once there, they are aided by Gilina, the Peacekeeper Tech Crichton and Aeryn encountered aboard the *Zelbinion* ("PK Tech Girl"). She's not only able to get Crichton past the DNA scan, but also manages to procure the cloned tissue sample that will save Aeryn's life.

Back on Moya, Aeryn is deteriorating rapidly. Using the leviathan's immune system to help flush the toxins out of her body, the crew keep a close watch on her. But everyone knows that time is running out.

On the Gammak Base, just when it seems everything is going smoothly, Crichton literally crosses paths with Scorpius, who senses Crichton's not what he seems and orders him seized. Crichton manages to hide the tissue sample before being captured and placed in the Aurora Chair, a terrible torture device which maps the mind's neural patterns and displays them. Scorpius believes Crichton is a spy on the same quest as Scorpius himself: The acquisition of wormhole technology. Crichton, of course, fears his comrades, including Gilina, will be discovered and captured.

While in the Chair, Crichton's memories reveal the contact with the Ancients from "A Human Reaction" and we learn at the same time Scorpius does that Crichton's unconscious mind possesses the data needed to create wormhole technology and that eventually he'll be able to access it intuitively.

Scorpius, determined to get the information he so desperately desires, pushes Crichton further and further until it seems that Crichton will either die or go mad. Eventually, Gilina and Chiana manage to contact Crichton in his cell. He tells them where the sample is located and Chiana, aided by Gilina, escapes on Aeryn's Prowler and returns to Moya.

Gilina, driven by her love for Crichton, is determined to help him, despite the fact that he's risking his life to save Aeryn, which causes her some emotional confusion. Aeryn recovers thanks to the tissue sample, but is devastated to discover Crichton missing.

CRITIQUE:

A good start to the four-part ending, this episode is well-paced and action packed. Chiana and Crichton have the most screen time and we get to observe just how well the two characters — as well as the two actors — work together. Chiana is definitely Crichton's best ally here as she knows how to play the game of getting information in exchange for a little flirtation and ego-boosting.

Introducing Scorpius, who is a much more powerful and frightening enemy than Crais could ever be, is a fine addition to the mythology arc of this series. The idea of the Aurora Chair is classic scifi — horrific and intriguing at the same time. The only problematic aspect of its presentation was that Crichton could see himself in his memories and in truth, this would not be possible.

The science behind the chair is sound — mapping the brain is already possible, although not to the extent the Chair allows. Memory is as individual as our personalities. The brain records memories in clusters, which is why a certain smell or image will trigger a memory.

Additionally, stimulating certain areas of the brain with electrical impulses can also trigger memory, but as yet, we don't have a screen on which to see them. Although the explanation in Crichton's Notes at the scifi channel's website claims that the Aurora Chair itself is what transposes the images from first to third person, it still feels like a choice made for viewer convenience.

For the most part up to this point, the writers have done a pretty good job with the women characters — they're smart, strong and capable, which is not always the case in scifi. Gilina is a perfect example of this: She's quick-thinking, willing to take chances and really knows her way around the Gammak Base's technical systems. Watching her work with Chiana is a real treat.

Although neither D'Argo, Zhaan nor Aeryn have much screen time here, the feeling of the ensemble is still present. Pulling out Crichton as the main focus is a usual strategy and is not unexpected. The cliff hanger ending keeps viewers on edge until the next installment.

ONE TIER BELOW:

- How can Scorpius tell that Crichton isn't Sebacean? Season Three's "Incubator" will answer that question.
- The fact that Gilina has been reposted to the Gammak Base indicates that PK Command may know of her encounter with Moya and her crew.
- Gilina's willingness to help Crichton and his friends adds interesting insight into PK culture. Aeryn's attitude toward techs, as you'll remember from "PK Tech Girl" wasn't a terribly positive one. Was Gilina born into the ranks to be a tech, engineered as Aeryn was for a life she didn't choose or was she,

like Bialar and his brother conscripted against her will? The fact that not all the members of the Peacekeepers are willing to follow orders is an intriguing bit of information which bears remembering.
- The fact that everyone agrees that saving Aeryn is more important than the risk involved is a crucial development in terms of integrating Aeryn into the crew. She has already proved her loyalty to them on several occasions. The choices made in this episode help strengthen the ties among Moya's crew.
- Watching Chiana work information out of the PK officers illustrates how she's been able to survive on her own without being captured or killed. Her willingness to use her sexuality to elicit information will become a point of conflict between her and the crew as the series progresses, although everyone is perfectly willing to let her help out in this instance.
- This episode introduces Stark, who is a member of a race we have not encountered before.
- Those interested in further exploration of memory and how it works might want to look at the classic non-fiction title *The Art of Memory* by Frances A. Yates and also *Hardboiled Wonderland and the End of the World*, a novel by Haruki Murakami.

Grade: A

Episode 10120: The Hidden Memory
Location: Hidden Peacekeeper Gammak Base
Guest Cast:
Gigi Edgley as Chiana
Lani Tupu as Captain Bialar Crais
Alyssa-Jane Cook as Gilina
Wayne Pygram as Scorpius
Paul Goddard as Stark
Imogen Annesley as Niem
Anthony Kierann as Lieutenant Heskon
Christian Bischoff as Bixx
Pete Walters as Crais' Guard
Nicole Roma as Blonde Technician
Writer: Justin Monjo
Director: Ian Watson

SYNOPSIS:

The second of four parts comprising Season One's final episodes, "The Hidden Memory" picks up where "Nerve" left off. Aeryn Sun has recovered and returns to the Gammak Base with D'Argo and Zhaan to rescue Crichton. While she searches for him, D'Argo and Zhaan wait on the roof, preparing the diversionary tactics which will hopefully get them away safely.

Meanwhile, Moya goes into labor and Pilot, Chiana and Rygel realize something quite frightening about Moya's offspring — he seems to have weaponry as part of his genetic makeup. As a result, he gets stuck in the birth canal. He begins to panic; Pilot fears he may open fire on Moya in an attempt to free himself. Chiana climbs into the birth canal and manages to free him without injuring either child or mother.

Down on the surface, Crichton and his cellmate

Stark bond over their shared experiences in the Aurora Chair. Contrary to Crichton's first impression, Stark is not insane, but uses madness as a survival tactic to divert Scorpius' attention. Stark confesses that he has no knowledge of wormhole technology, but is protecting a private memory from long ago in the deepest recesses of his mind. Because Stark is so protective of it, Scoripus assumes it contains wormhole technology and so has been bent on retrieving it.

But for now, Scorpius has other problems. He has been unable to break Crichton and even the arrival of Crichton's old nemesis Bialar Crais fails to convince Crichton to let down his mental walls. Gilina manages to swap out some of the Chair's components. When she tells Crichton that he *must* think of her, it triggers a set of false memories which are displayed for Crais and Scorpius.

Scorpius is duped by the false memories which implicate Crais as possessor of information about wormhole technology. Crichton is returned to his cell and Scorpius puts Crais in the Chair instead. There Scorpius learns Crais has disobeyed orders to pursue Crichton. But he also discovers that he's been tricked. Crais has no hidden memories.

By this time, Aeryn has managed to free Crichton and Stark and they make their way to the roof where a firefight ensues between Peackeeper troops and the prisoners. Gilina, knowing her subterranean refuge will be discovered, decides to accompany Crichton and the others, but is mortally wounded during the escape.

Safely aboard Moya once more, Stark gifts Gilina with his hidden memory and helps her crossover into death. The crew, along with the newborn leviathan, flee the Gammak Base with Crais and Scorpius in pursuit.

CRITIQUE:

The second part of this finale had a more even distribution between ensemble members, though D'Argo and Zhaan still don't have as much screen time as the others. The narrative bounces effectively between the multiple storylines, heightening tension and raising more questions along the way.

Throwing Crais into the mix here is a great choice, especially when Scorpius is fooled into believing that Crais knows more than he does. Now Crichton has two mortal enemies, but Scorpius is definitely the more dangerous, possessing a keen intellect and a complete lack of scruples. Mr. Pygram's portrayal of this character is remarkable. From his vocal inflections to his movements and expressions, the character is engaging, frightening and definitely ups the ante. Crichton can't keep himself or his friends out of trouble. It's interesting to see how badly the Human fares when pitted against alien cultures. Crichton's not stupid, nor is he just the Average Joe, but he's clearly out of his depth here and it's interesting to think about how any Human might manage in his situation.

Alyssa-Jane Cooke does a fine turn in Gilina's final episode, once again using her intelligence and technical abilities to free Crichton. Although portrayed as emotionally naïve, it's clear that she comes to understand what has transpired between John and Aeryn since her encounter with Crichton on the *Zelbinion*.

Since much hype was given to the fact that someone would die during the four-part finale, it seemed pretty clear it would be Gilina once we saw her in "Nerve." In truth, in order for the Aeryn/Cichton relationship arc to continue, Gilina has to be reintroduced and then killed off. Unfortunately, her death really isn't given the emotional screen time it deserves. It leaves us to wonder whether Crichton realizes that she's given her life so he can escape. He seems too willing to gloss over her death as though it's a given. This really cheats the depth of Ms. Cooke's performance and the relationship between the two characters.

Stark is a fascinating addition to the show's alien roster. In what is fast becoming *Farscape* tradition, is another unique alien. The bright light where half his head should be, the beautiful memory he's hidden for so long that he's able to give to Gilina, the intelligence hidden behind madness makes him stand out from the other characters even though he is a supporting player.

Some other questions arise about how secret this base really is. Scorpius transmits the coordinates to Crais in "Nerve" without a second thought and both Crais and Aeryn seem familiar with the Aurora Chair (Crais knew no captain had ever been forced into it and Aeryn recognized the controls) — how could that be possible if Crais had been essentially out of the loop for close to a cycle and Scorpius' work is top secret?

Additionally, there are some glaring continuity errors — watch Stark essentially teleport from one side of the room to the other in one scene and Chiana and Rygel travel several levels on Moya in the space of one spoken line. It's implied that Zhaan's planting bombs to stop the Peacekeepers from using the lift, but they manage to gain access to the rooftop anyway and the bombs don't explode until Crichton sets an additional charge.

The birth of Moya's offspring, though it has been the motivation for many choices during this season, is strangely underplayed here. Although everyone is grateful that Moya and child are well, there is little sense of celebration or joy at the leviathan's birth. Given the fact that so much time and energy has been devoted to this storyline, the way it's played seems odd.

Overall though, the episode is well paced and opens other doors for future conflicts, shifting alliances and much more.

ONE TIER BELOW:

- Stark has a gift which helps an individual cross over into death. For another take on this ability, check out the character Elmer in Morgan and Wong's unfortunately short-lived series *The Others*.
- Why does Moya's offspring have weaponry as part of his natural physiology?
- How do leviathans breed? If they're hermaphrodites, how was her DNA altered to produce such an unusual child?

Grade: A

Episode 10121: Bone to Be Wild
Location: Asteroid Field
Guest Cast:
Gigi Edgley as Chiana
Lani Tupu as Captain Bialar Crais
Wayne Pygram as Scorpius
David Franklin as Lieutenant Braca
Francesca Buller as M'Lee
Marton Csokas as Br'Nee
Writer: David Kemper and Rockne O'Bannon
Director: Andrew Prowse

SYNOPSIS:

In the third part of the season finale, Moya and crew have run deeper into the asteroid field in an attempt to escape from Scorpious and the Peacekeepers. As they lower Moya's temperature to lower the energy signatures, everyone becomes cranky with the cold. They receive a distress call from a small habitable asteroid and decide to investigate. Crichton, D'Argo and Zhaan take one of the transport pods down to the surface. There, they encounter two life forms: Br'Nee, a botanist; and M'Lee, an enigmatic individual who claims Br'Nee is trying to kill her.

While Crichton, D'Argo and Zhaan try and sort out the truth, Aeryn boards Moya's offspring and begins to engage with him. Afraid he'll become startled and break from Moya's side, thus endangering the entire crew as well as both leviathans, Aeryn works to form a trusting bond.

Aboard the Peacekeeper Command Carrier, Crais is falling further and further out of favor with Scorpious. It becomes clear that Crais is in danger of losing his commission as well as his command position on the ship, especially now that Scorpious knows he disobeyed orders to pursue Crichton into the Uncharted Territories.

Planetside, the crew eventually sorts out what's what: Br'Nee's people brought M'Lee's people (who need large doses of calcium to survive) to the planet to "consume" all of the fauna so the flora the botanists wanted to study and cultivate would be able to flourish. Unfortunately, no one considered the fact — or if it was considered no one wanted to make provisions — that eventually the food source M'Lee's people needed to survive would run out. They would turn not only on Br'Nee and his company, but also resort to cannibalizing their own in order to survive.

Zhaan, initially astounded and ecstatic about discovering a world so rich in plant life which can be used for healing purposes, is coveted by Br'Nee — not because of her knowledge, but because of the fact that Zhaan herself is ... a plant. He plots to get her alone with him and then using a miniaturizing laser, turns her into a Zhaan action figure and puts her in a jar.

Crichton manages to figure out the twisted and contradictory stories and not only restores Zhaan to her previous proportions, but also "accidentally" kills Br'Nee, thus providing M'Lee with a temporary food source.

Before departing, the crew promise that a larger food source will soon arrive. And at the episode's end, it does, in the form of Scorpious and company. As he embraces her, charmed as we were initially by her helpless demeanor and intriguing story, we can only hope that he'll fall prey to some version of the giant's chant from *Jack in the Beanstalk* and she'll grind his bones to make her bread.

CRITIQUE:

Taken as the third of four parts in Season One's much-heralded Season Finale, this episode is the weakest link. It is, in *The X-Files* terminology, a monster episode stuck in the middle of a powerful mythology arc. While "Nerve" and "The Hidden Memory" are focused and well-paced, this episode suffered from some bad choices both in terms of writing and editing.

The biggest problem is that the writer is trying to cover too much ground. There are too many plot threads and the result is a tangled skein. Crichton wastes time running back and forth, using his brawn instead of his brain to figure things out. Since he's clearly a smart fellow, it's insulting to see him portrayed as slow-witted. D'Argo has some great lines in the episode's opening scenes, but is then reduced to serving as an anchor for Crichton's mad dashes between the transport pod and the outside world. D'Argo's only other purpose in this episode is to tell M'Lee there will be more "food" arriving shortly. While important information, this episode does not further his character development in any way. So far in the season finale, he's been completely wasted.

The revelation of Zhaan's plant-ness is wonderful, as is her exchange with Crichton in which she calls him an animal-centric jerk. What is really great about this dialogue is that initially, we may find ourselves agreeing with Crichton and then experience a rude awakening when Zhaan points out the flaw in his logic.

Zhaan's disappearing act in the face of Br'Nee's

initial arrival was visually intriguing. But how did she get her clothes to disappear with her? The underlying insidious nature of Br'Nee's motivations raise some difficult questions, ones we mere Humans wrestle with in various forms: Should we experiment on animals to develop drug treatments for Humans? Should we use pesticides to allow certain kinds of flora to flourish while endangering or eliminating other forms of life? What kinds of ethics should guide research of any kind involving sentient beings? All hard questions. All important ones. This episode could have been a powerful way to explore these issues if it had been developed separately rather than sandwiched into the season finale.

The same is true for the continued development of Crais' falling from Peacekeeper grace and Scorpious' rise to power, and all the scenes involving Chiana or Rygel. They're stories become nothing more than background noise which dilutes the intense focus we've had for the previous two episodes.

The most moving sequences involving Aeryn and the offspring's initial contacts are almost completely lost. Ms. Black does a fantastic job here interacting with the hybrid leviathan-gunship and we are treated to a sneak peek of this character's potential. Since so many decisions the crew made were based upon the safety and continuing development of Moya's child, it's really too bad the writers didn't move this to the forefront of the episode. This offspring's birth, his potential, his genetic background are all so incredibly fascinating and yet despite the time given to this story arc in season one, it's relegated to a sub-plot.

Continuity questions arise as well. How do Crais and Scorpius know about Moya's offspring if he was born during Crichton's imprisonment? Crichton would have no memories of the birth to be ripped from him in the Chair. If they spotted the offspring during pursuit of Moya, why didn't they just destroy Moya? Where is Stark? Additionally, the crew could not have survived if the heat on Moya had really been turned off completely, despite the cozy parkas. And probably most puzzling was the explanation that all the fauna on the asteroid has been destroyed. If that was true, how were the plants pollinated? Br'Nee could not possibly have pollinated them all by hand.

If this episode had focused simply on the planetside story, it would have been great. The makeup department outdid themselves here with Br'Nee and M'Lee. The changing colors on M'Lee's headpiece, her extending spines, and overall presentation were incredible. Br'Nee's multiple faces, his general bearing, his hands and even the mushrooms growing out of his head were inventive, fun and intriguing. Francesca Buller's portrayal of M'Lee was also phenomenal. Like Ms. Edgley, Ms. Buller completely embodies her character (no pun intended) and uses movement, speech and expression to create a unique and fascinating addition to the alien races Crichton — and by extension the audience — has been exposed to.

Taken alone, the story is also interesting and its resolution satisfying. But spliced into the existing mythology arc involving Crais, the offspring, Scorpius and the wormhole technology, it was a jarring and unsatisfying section of the four-part sequence.

ONE TIER BELOW:

- There were several clues about Zhaan which were planted (pardon the pun) during the course of this

season. In "Throne for a Loss" we see that her blood is white and has healing properties. She's also able to puncture her skin without causing much damage. Much like an aloe, whose leaves contain a salve which eases minor burns, Zhaan is a healer on more levels than one. In "Till the Blood Runs Clear," the photogasms she experiences appear to be the result of accelerated or intensified photosynthesis. "Rhapsody in Blue" reveals the tree Crichton chops down to be an integral part of a plant culture, but this metaphor isn't clear until now. It makes perfect sense for people who are plants to have a plant as an object in which power resides.
- When asked in an online chat what kind of plant Zhaan is, Ms. Hey replied that she's a succulent. ;)
- Francesca Buller is Ben Browder's wife. This is her first of several guest appearances on the show.
- This is the first time that Scorpius' right hand man, Lieutenant Braca is introduced.

Grade: C- (as part of the four-part Season Finale)
Grade: B (as a stand-alone monster episode)

Episode 10122: Family Ties
Location: Near the Peacekeeper Gammak Base
Guest Cast:
Gigi Edgley as Chiana
Lani Tupu as Captain Bialar Crais
Wayne Pygram as Scorpius
Writer: David Kemper and Rockne S. O'Bannon
Director: Tony Tilse

SYNOPSIS:

While Crais and Scorpius comb the asteroid field for Moya, Rygel comes to the realization that Crichton might actually be worth something. Hoping to trade Crichton for transport back to Hyneria, Rygel steals a pod and is taken aboard the Command Carrier.

After stating his demands and eating enough to fill his three stomachs, Rygel is immersed in a relaxing bath when he sees one of Crais' trophies: The bloody head of a former Hynerian prisoner. Crais arrives and informs Rygel that his plan is flawed and Scorpius intends a slow and painful death for him. Crais, looking disheveled and shaken, makes Rygel an offer he can't refuse: Crais agrees to help Rygel escape in exchange for asylum aboard Moya.

Rygel returns to Moya with Crais, much to the shock of the others. Crais is shut into a cell and Crichton berates him for the stress he's caused. Crais admits he knows Tauvo's death was an accident.

After discussing and discarding several plans to evade or destroy the Command Carrier, the crew finally agrees to send D'Argo and Crichton toward the Gammak Base with a load of explosives. They will jump ship at the last possible moment, and then Aeryn, hovering nearby in her Prowler, will scoot in and pick them up before D'Argo loses consciousness.

The plan runs smoothly for about thirty microts. The Command Carrier breaks off its pursuit of Moya to go after the pod but soon turn their attention back to Moya. Meanwhile, Aeryn is unable to pick up Crichton and D'Argo because of the presence of other Prowlers in the area. The pod explodes, destroying the base. Then, to complicate matters, Crais steals the offspring. With the baby gone and Aeryn, Crichton and D'Argo in a waiting game, Moya is forced to starburst in order to save those still on board. The last image we have is of D'Argo losing consciousness and his hand opening to release Jack Crichton's ring into the vacuum of space.

CRITIQUE:

As a season finale, this episode was satisfying, creating a number of scenarios which will be resolved in Season Two.

We are also given some of Aeryn's backstory. Before Crichton departs, Aeryn tells him of a scarred and seasoned warrior who visited Aeryn's bedside when she was a child. Crichton assumes it was her father and we get a good laugh when Aeryn gives him one of her incredulous looks and says it was her mother. Aeryn tells Crichton that as as opposed to being bred purely to fill the ranks, she was conceived out of love. But all she knows about her parents is that her father's name was Talyn and that her mother visited her on this one occasion. Aeryn, who had been chosen by the offspring to provide him with a name, decides to call him after the father she never knew.

Additionally, Crais tries to bond with Aeryn over

Talyn, reminding her that they are both without family. While Aeryn insists that Talyn should stay with Moya, Crais implies that Talyn will be fine on his own. He seems anxious to learn everything about Talyn and it's hard to tell where his loyalties lie until he hijacks the leviathan.

There were some holes in the story, though, and some of the characters really get pushed aside as the plot takes precedence. Chiana's only real contribution to this episode is making everyone's favorite dishes, although how she does this — and how she knows — is something of a mystery since it seems they're always short on food. Additionally, the writers are lazy with Chiana. Is all she can offer the crew is either sex or food? Are we to conclude that if she can't screw Crichton, she'll cook for everybody instead. So much for breaking stereotypes of women in scifi.

Why, if there is a risk that Aeryn might not get to D'Argo in time, don't they take a spacesuit for him? Surely there must have been some tall Peacekeepers on board Moya at one time or another. There seems to be an endless supply of weapons and PK clothing ... again, as a ratings ploy this worked but it was a red herring in the logic of the story.

So at the end of Season One, the crew has been splintered: Aeryn waits in her Prowler; Crichton and D'Argo are floating in space with a limited survival time; Crais has stolen Talyn; Zhaan, Chiana, Rygel and Moya have starburst to another part of the Uncharted Territories. Scorpius is still in pursuit of Crichton — although why he doesn't have what he needs from Crichton by now is a mystery. Since he was able to uncover the information given Crichton about wormhole technology why wasn't he able to retrieve it?

The first twenty-two episodes, taken as a body of work, provide some intriguing material. Fans of the show have come to identify with the characters, many picking their favorites from among the show's core ensemble. The explosion of websites and postings reflects *Farscape*'s growing popularity. Hopefully, the creative team of writers, directors and actors will continue to take risks and produce a well-acted, entertaining and engaging science fiction television experience.

ONE TIER BELOW:

- The ring Jack Crichton gives to his son in the first episode appears again here.
- Aeryn's memory of her mother will become an important aspect of a major story arc in Season Three.
- When Crais arrives on Moya, D'Argo severely beats him, resulting in Crais' admission that D'Argo's imprisonment was politically motivated. In front of the rest of the crew, Crais says D'Argo was not responsible for his wife's death.
- For viewers in the States, this cliffhanger aired just before a break, but those in Britain got to see the first episode of Season Two, "Mind the Baby," the next week.
- Why doesn't Crichton's favorite meal appear on the table with everyone else's?
- What are Crais' motivations? Has he become an ally? Does he steal Talyn to keep him away from Scorpius, or is he acting selfishly?
- What does Crais want from Aeryn? Is he in love with her or does he just find her sexually attractive?

Does he think their shared PK background will be enough to forge a bond between them?
- Since Crais has abandon his Command Carrier, will he also be exiled from the Peacekeepers and declared contaminated? Is his defection a planned move?
- Why has Crais continued to pursue Crichton and the others if he knows that Tauvo's death was an accident?
- Will Talyn require a symbiotic pilot? How is Crais able to maneuver the leviathan without a pilot on board?

Grade: A-

Grade Point Average for Season One: B

On to Season Two!

Author Biography

Talis Pelucir lives with his wife and children near Ullswater, England. He has written more than a dozen books for Lightning Rod Publishers, many of which are listed on the last page of this episode guide.

About Windstorm Creative
and our Readers' Club

Windstorm Creative was founded in 1989 to create a publishing house with author-centric ethics and cutting-edge, risk-taking innovation. WSC is now a company of more than ten divisions with international distribution channels that allow us to sell our books — paperback and hardcover — games, music and films both inside the traditional systems and outside these paradigms, capitalizing on more direct delivery and non-traditional markets. As a result, our books can be found in grocery superstores as well as your favorite neighborhood bookstore, and dozens of other outlets on and off the Internet.

WSC is an independent press with the synergy and branding of a corporate publisher and an author royalty that's easily twice their best offer. We have continued to minimize returns without decreasing sales by publishing books that are timeless, as opposed to timely, and never back-listing our books. We stand adamantly against the heinous act of "stripping."

WSC is constantly changing, improving, and growing. We are driven by the needs of our authors – hailing from ten different countries – and the vision of our critically-acclaimed staff. All of our books are created with the strictest of environmental protections in mind. Our approach to no-waste, no-hazard, in-house production, and stringent out-source scrutiny, assures that our goals are met whether books are printed at our own facility or an outside press.

Because of these precautions, our books cost more. And though we know that our readers support our efforts, we also understand that a few dollars can add up. This is why we began our Readers' Club. Visit our webcenter and take 20% off every title, every day, by typing in the code found at the bottom of the page. No strings. No fine print.

While you're at our site, feel free to preview or request the first chapter of any of our titles, completely free of charge.

Thank you for supporting an independent press.

Readers' Club code #73564TP
www.windstormcreative.com
and click on Shop
See next page for title recommendations.

The Farscape Episode Guide for Season Two: Aeryn's PK past returns to haunt her. D'Argo receives news of his son from an unlikely source. Chiana reveals the reason she was exiled from Nebari Prime. Zhaan is sentenced to life in prison for jaywalking. Crichton and Aeryn find out they're "compatible," and Scorpius' search for John and the wormhole technology continues. Plus the return of some favorite characters from Season One, including enigmatic Captain Crais.

The Farscape Episode Guide for Season Three: Two Crichtons! Twice the fun. Season Three cranks up the heat between John and Aeryn while delivering a number of new surprises. Scorpy's backstory! Zhaan's sacrifice! New cast members. New episodes.

The Farscape Episode Guide for Season Four: It's over?! No!! Talis reviews the final season's wonders and blunders — what *are* those little pieces floating around in the water?!

Farscape! The Best Websites and Factoids: Looking for the best Farscape websites? Let Lightning Rod point you in the right direction. You're tired of aimlessly searching the web. You're sick of garbled search engine descriptions. You've tried checking out webrings but what good are they if half the sites offer the same information? Our guides list names, URL addresses and concise descriptions of the best sites on a topic. We only list the best-designed, most easily navigated and most easily understood sites that offer unique or exclusive information. The text in the guide is in a clear, large font for easy reading and copying into any web browser. Plus, you'll find great factoids right here without ever having to sign on! Vital information and fascinating facts about your favorite topic. For newbies and experts alike, we give you factoids that everyone should know or be reminded of. No rumors here — just the better-than-fiction facts. Lightning Rod guides are compiled by fans, not computers. Regularly updated and revised, guides are simple, straight-forward and unofficial.

Other Titles by Talis Pelucir: Babylon 5! The Best Websites and Factoids; Babylon 5: Crusade! The Best Websites and Factoids; Star Trek: The Original Series! The Best Websites and Factoids; The X-Files! The Best Websites and Factoids; Buffy the Vampire Slayer! The Best Websites and Factoids; The Pokémon The Best Websites and Factoids; Gillian Anderson! The Best Websites; Sandra Bullock! The Best Websites, and many, many more!